COMPLETE BOOK OF
Gymnastics

Newton C. Loken

Gymnastic Coach, University of Michigan

Robert J. Willoughby

Gymnastic Coach, Eastern Michigan University

PRENTICE-HALL, INC.

Englewood Cliffs, N.J.

PRENTICE-HALL PHYSICAL EDUCATION SERIES
Elmer D. Mitchell, *Editor*

Library of Congress Catalog Card No. 59-9044

Sixth printing........June, 1961

PRINTED IN THE UNITED STATES OF AMERICA

15715-C

Dedicated

TO THE ENTHUSIASTIC AND LOYAL GYMNASTIC PAR-
ticipants, coaches, teachers and fans who have supported the revival of the sport of gymnastics to its
rightful place alongside the other fine sports of our
schools, clubs and colleges throughout the country.

Foreword

DURING THE PAST TEN YEARS I have had the pleasure of observing the teaching of the authors. Both have demonstrated that they are genuine students and master teachers of Gymnastics. Newt Loken and Robert Willoughby have learned their Gymnastics as performers, teachers and coaches. The former was honored by his colleagues in the coaching field by being elected President of the National Gymnastic Coaches Association. Their experiences and writings attest to their qualifications. It is only logical that their combined talents could be channelled into writing a useful compendium in the field of Gymnastics. I take pleasure and pride in commending to teachers and coaches this work, *Complete Book of Gymnastics*, by Newt Loken and Robert Willoughby.

Paul Hunsicker, *Chairman*
Department of Physical Education
University of Michigan

Preface

WITH THE RECENT NATIONWIDE SURGE of interest in physical fitness, there has been a campaign for the inclusion of more gymnastics in our physical education curricula. It has been found that development of the upper body has been inadequate and that gymnastics makes a unique contribution toward overcoming this lack. With this in mind, many schools throughout the country are dusting off apparatus that has stood in storage rooms, seldom used. But now that this equipment is on the floor once again, we find that many instructors are not qualified to teach this activity.

Nearly everyone has seen acrobats perform in circuses or in films. Many have witnessed competitive gymnastics as performed by accomplished gymnasts in colleges or in A.A.U. meets. Few, however, realize all that has transpired to produce this high level of performance. All of these expert performers had to start at the elementary level and be taught solid fundamentals by an instructor, either in an organized class or informally in small groups. Certainly every physical education instructor is not expected to be a gymnastic coach and produce experts, but he should know how to teach the beginning and intermediate levels

of this activity. This then is a challenge to all teacher-training institutions to provide basic instruction in gymnastics.

Several books have been written covering one or two specific areas within the total gymnastic field. These books usually cover their subject matter thoroughly from the elementary stunts through the advanced levels. There are very few books, however, that include the whole field of gymnastics under one cover. Therefore, it is the purpose of this book to:

1. Cover adequately gymnastic instruction for both men and women at the beginning, intermediate, and even advanced levels of gymnastic skills.

2. Include in one book the complete range of gymnastics, plus such allied activities as calisthenics, rope skipping, rope climbing, and exhibitions.

To do this, we have not exhausted all of the stunts that could be performed in each event, but instead have selected the ones which we feel adequately cover the elementary and intermediate skill levels. Along with this we have tried to present the material in a manner suitable for class instruction.

Good luck, good spotting, and good performances!

ACKNOWLEDGMENTS

We are indebted to many individuals who have contributed greatly to the development of this book. Those who contributed specific material used in some of the chapters are:

Dr. James Baley, Professor of Physical Education, Mississippi Southern College, Hattiesburg, Mississippi (*Balancing*).

Gordon Hathaway, Exeter Schools, New Hampshire (*Rope Activities*).

Herb Loken, Gymnastic Coach, Bakersfield College, Bakersfield, California (*Side Horse*).

Jess Meyers, Lanier High School, West Alexandria, Ohio (*Exhibitions*).

Dr. Otto Ryser, Gymnastic Coach, Indiana University, Bloomington, Indiana (*Calisthenics*).

Bob Sullivan, Gymnastic Coach, Air Force Academy, Colorado Springs, Colorado (*Tumbling*).

Erna Wachtel, Past Olympic Women's Coach, Chicago (*Women's Chapters*).

Sincere appreciation is expressed to Colonel Ted Bank of the Athletic Institute for the use of the many fine pictures throughout the book. These pictures came from four new gymnastic films produced by his company. Thanks also to Dallas Jones and his staff for the fine work on the pictures and parts of the descriptions.

We thank Neil Mattinen for his excellent drawings of the women's vaulting and also George Gulack, Chairman, National A.A.U., for permission to use them.

The *Athletic Journal*, *Scholastic Coach* and the *Journal of Health, Physical Education and Recreation* very graciously allowed us to use pictures from their files.

Our deepest thanks to Dr. Elmer D. Mitchell for his constant encouragement and support throughout this lengthy project. Appreciation is extended to Ray Chinn and to Ed Gagnier for their thoughts and opinions regarding descriptions and selections of stunts.

A special note of thanks to the many fine performers who are pictured throughout the book. These include: Ed Cole (Big Ten and N.C.A.A. Trampoline Champion), Dick Kimball (Midwest Trampoline Champion), Nino Marion (N.C.A.A. Still Rings Runner-Up Champion), Richard Montpetit (Canadian All-Around Champion), Jim Brown and Bill Skinner (Tumbling Champions), Tom Francis and Tony Turner (outstanding divers and tumblers), and Carolyn Osborn (champion woman gymnast).

Contents

CHAPTER 1

History and Values

of Gymnastics

HISTORY

GYMNASTICS AND TUMBLING, comprising some of our most basic motor skills, also include some of the oldest skills. Their beginnings are somewhat obscure, but they possibly began about 2600 B.C. when the Chinese developed a few activities that resembled gymnastics, particularly of the medical type. However, real development of gymnastics began in the Grecian and Roman periods of history. The Greeks first gave great emphasis to gymnastics; in fact, the word itself is derived from the Greek. Systematic exercise received endorsement from the most eminent educators of ancient times and it became a prominent feature in the state regulations for education. In fact, the period spent for gymnastics was equal to the time spent on art and music combined. The Spartans were most rigid in providing gymnastic training for their youth. Girls also were expected to be good gymnasts. The exercises consisted of various tumbling, dancing, running, leaping, rope-climbing and balance movements.

The early Romans copied the physical training program from the Greeks but adapted it to their military training program. With the fall of the Greek and Roman civilizations, gymnastics declined. In fact, all forms of physical activity were discouraged. This was true throughout the Middle Ages and into the Renaissance, when a renewed surge of interest in systematic physical activity swept the European countries. Perhaps the earliest contributor to this renewed interest was Johann Basedow (1723-1790) of Germany who in 1776 added gymnastic exercises to the program of instruction in his school. Johann Guts Muths (1759-1893), who is known as the "great-grandfather of gymnastics," introduced gymnastics into the Prussian schools. He wrote several works on the subject, including *Gymnastics for Youth*, said to be the first book on gymnastics. The real "father of gymnastics" was Friedrich Jahn (1778-1852). Jahn, who is regarded as the founder of the *Turnverein*, conceived the idea of combining gymnastic training with patriotic demonstrations. This was received very well by

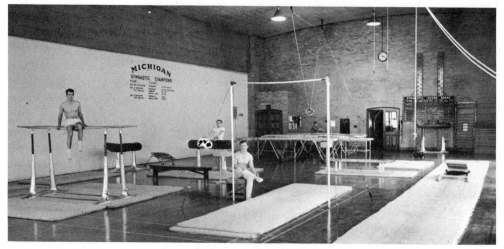

A gymnastics room

the government and thus the program grew rapidly involving huge playgrounds and whole families participating. Jahn invented several pieces of equipment, among them the horizontal bar, parallel bars, side horse, and vaulting buck. Later when threat of war subsided, Jahn's motives were misunderstood and the authorities had him jailed for planning to overthrow the government. The *Turnvereinen* societies then moved into closed buildings for protection where they still function in Europe and the United States.

Adolf Spiess (1810-1858) is responsible for introducing gymnastics into the schools of Switzerland.

Pehr Ling (1776-1839) of Sweden was the first to appreciate the corrective value of gymnastics. He simplified the exercises for use by the individual. Ling invented the equipment known today as Swedish apparatus, including the stall bars and the vaulting box.

Franz Nachtegall (1777-1847) started the first school for training gymnastics teachers at Copenhagen.

The development of gymnastics in America began with physical education programs patterned after European pro-

grams. This European influence was felt greatly through the Turnverein movement. When the Turners organization felt the need for training instructors for its numerous clubs, it established in 1865 the Normal College of American Gymnastics in Indianapolis, Indiana. For years this college turned out superb instructors in gymnastics and related activities.

One of the first American contributors to gymnastics was Dr. Dudley Sargent. While still a student he became a teacher of gymnastics at Bowdoin College. Within two years he had developed the activity as an official part of the regular college curriculum. He later served at Yale before moving to Harvard where he became Director of the Hemenway Gymnasium. During his life Dr. Sargent invented many pieces of apparatus, including such items as pulley weights and leg and finger machines. He also developed a system of anthropometric measurements for determining the physical condition of the student.

The YMCA's also made a very notable contribution to the gymnastic program in the USA with their encouragement and inclusion of the activity in their programs. They installed apparatus in their gymnasia and provided instruction in gymnastics at their training school at Springfield, Massachusetts. One of their early leaders who became prominent in the movement of physical training along educational lines was Dr. Luther Gulick.

In the World War II physical training programs, renewed emphasis on gymnastics and tumbling resulted in increased growth of the activity in our schools after the war. Within the last decade, there has been a phenomenal surge of interest in the sport. Old gymnastic centers like Philadelphia, Minneapolis, and Los Angeles are still active, and many new areas produce an energetic flow of top-notch gymnastic coaches, teams, and fans. This is especially true of the Chicago suburban area. The National Collegiate Gymnastic Meet is now a very large affair attracting many top-flight teams, while a short time ago there were only a few schools entered. Clinics have sprung up throughout the country, highlighted by the annual Sarasota (Florida) Clinic. The Sarasota Clinic, started in the winter of 1951, has grown from a small beginning to become a very big attraction. The Board of Directors has included Lyle Welser, Tom Maloney, Ed Scrobe, Frank Cumiskey, and Frank Wells, with competent clinic personnel in such people as George Szypula, Ralph Piper, Gene Wettstone, Newt Loken, and Bud Beyer.

The very active and functional National Association of Gymnastic Coaches was formed in 1950 by a small group of gymnastic coaches led by Chet Phillips. Past Presidents of the Association are: Phillips, Pond, Welser, Maloney, Charles Keeney, Szypula, Loken, and Hal Frey. In 1955, the NAGC adopted a policy of honoring one person each year who has made an outstanding contribution to gymnastics over a period of 25 years or more. The first five so honored were Max Younger, Roy E. Moore, Hartley Price, Leslie Judd, and Gus Heineman. In 1959, plans were being made to have gymnastics represented in the nationally famous Helms Hall of Fame. George Szypula headed a committee to nominate candidates for this award.

In 1959, the Wheaties Sports Federation inaugurated plans for promoting the All-American Teams of ten sports, including gymnastics. The All-American Selection Board with Newt Loken as chairman included the Past Presidents of the NAGC, along with Joe E. Brown, the actor, as Honorary Member.

Obviously, a great deal is happening in gymnastics. It is being rediscovered that, with proper supervision and instruction, gymnastics can be one of the most popular and exciting activities in the school program.

GENERAL VALUES

What are some of the contributions which gymnastics makes to the development of the individual? Recent studies involving physical fitness indicate that gymnastics should be a vital activity in physical fitness training. The movements in this activity are fundamentally big muscle movements and will develop greatly the muscle groups in the arms, shoulders, chest, and abdomen. These areas of the body are often neglected in other sports. Tumbling and trampolining also develop the musculature of the legs. Besides building up strength and power, gymnastics also contributes to other factors of physical fitness such as agility, flexibility, coordination, and balance. A general improvement in posture also can be derived from this type of activity.

Gymnastics has special meaning as a sport. The emphasis is placed on co-ordination and skill. Students whose capabilities and size may not fit them for contact sports can find in gymnastics satisfaction of competition and the thrill of accomplishment in skillful physical activity.

In addition to these physical factors, gymnastics also develops such mental qualities as alertness, daring, and precision. Split-second timing is necessary in many of the stunts which call for quick thinking. Since gymnastics is an individual sport, the gymnast is the only person who can make himself overcome his fears in learning new stunts. Upon repetition of stunts the gymnast develops habits of definite decisions and actions which must be correct for the successful completion of the stunt.

Such character traits as self-confidence, perseverance, and self-discipline are developed from gymnastic activities. If the gymnast works to make progress, he quickly learns that he must develop perseverance to the highest degree. He must apply self-discipline and force himself to try repeatedly the same stunt until mastery is finally accomplished. Because gymnastics is a self-testing activity each individual may progress at his own speed. A gymnast who is challenged by a particular advanced stunt or routine is not prevented from trying it by the lack of progress of his fellow gymnast.

Creative ability has unlimited opportunity in the sport of gymnastics. Great pleasure is derived from working out possible combinations and routines. This develops in the gymnast an understanding of symmetry, continuity, coordination, balance, and timing. It also develops an understanding of the need for strength and endurance in order to complete some of the created routines set up by the gymnast.

Another contribution is the fun and enjoyment received from participating in the activity. The joy of successfully completing a stunt is outstanding. The elation of learning a handspring, kip or giant swing is indescribable. To see children laughing and shouting with joy and pride as they successfully complete a stunt is indeed rewarding to the gymnastic instructor.

CHAPTER 2

Calisthenics

EVERYONE DOES CALISTHENICS every day, whether he is aware of it or not. In the very process of cleaning house, working in the yard, or just walking, one performs exercises that are similar to those in calisthenics. However, most people do not do enough exercise or enough of the right kind to gain the benefits of health that may be theirs. The term, "calisthenics," is derived from Greek words meaning "beautiful strength," and implies light free exercises in contrast to the vigorous exercises using apparatus, usually known as "gymnastics."

VALUES

The specific values of calisthenics are:

1. It is important for a person to be thoroughly warmed up before participating in strenuous activity such as is found in most sports. Calisthenic exercises can provide this warm-up if well chosen.

2. Calisthenics also play a big part in long-range conditioning of athletes

Calisthenics in action

for participation in sports. Other groups, such as ballet and modern dancers, employ calisthenics to develop suppleness and endurance.

3. Perhaps the greatest value of calisthenics is its contribution to physical fitness. This is important not only in school-aged children but also in adults. With the widespread attention being given to the poor physical fitness of America's children, this type of activity might warrant a more prominent place in the physical education program.

4. Included in the physical fitness merits is the carry-over value of calisthenics. For the last 20 or 30 years we've been hearing and reading about the necessity of teaching sports with carry-over value. Tennis, badminton, handball, and golf are all mentioned as activities of this nature. But what about calisthenics? Five to ten minutes of bending and twisting or other simple exercises every morning can help to keep men and women in good health and help them to feel fit throughout the day. Of course it will not counteract the ill effects of over-indulgence in eating, smoking, drinking and lack of sleep, but it will stimulate circulation, increase the respiratory rate, and pep up the appetite. All this tends to give one a feeling of well being and a brighter outlook on life.

5. The last but certainly not the least value of calisthenics is found in rehabilitation programs. Such programs employ special types of exercises to counteract malformations or to strengthen muscles which have been weakened through disuse.

ORGANIZATION

Space is not of prime importance for calisthenics. An outdoor area, large or small, can be used. A gymnasium of any size is adequate and when this is unavailable, even hallways or classrooms are feasible.

Arrangement of Class

When using calisthenics for a gymnasium period, keep these rules in mind when planning the arrangement of the class.

1. Students should be placed so that they can all see the instructor.
2. The instructor should be able to see all of the students.
3. Students should be far enough apart so that they will not interfere with each other's movements.

There are scores of ways to get the class into such an order; only a few will be mentioned here. It is well to vary the method from time to time to avoid monotony and stereotyped responses.

1. *At Will.* The most informal and probably the fastest way of accomplishing the job is to tell the class members to fall out into open order. At the command, each individual steps forward into the assigned area, extends his arms sideward and swings them around in an arc to make sure that he will not interfere with anyone else while exercising. Each individual adjusts his position as needed and comes to attention when satisfied with his spot. This is not so easily accomplished as might seem, especially if the students are rather young or if the class is not well controlled.

2. *Numbers on Floor.* Spots or numbers on the floor at proper intervals may facilitate the assembling of the class. If numbers are to be used, each child can be assigned a specific number on which he is to stand. This device can also be used to take the roll. The teacher need only note and record the unoccupied numbers to find out who is absent.

3. *Count Off.* Another commonly used procedure is to line the class up in a straight line, have them count off by fours (fives, sixes, and so on, depending on the size of the class and the size of the area) and have each person take twice as many steps forward as his number. Thus, the number fours will take eight steps forward, the number threes will take six steps, and so on. This method is fast, accurate, lends itself to maintaining control over the class and can be used outdoors or in other places where spots or numbers on the floor are not feasible.

4. *Variety.* It is not always necessary that the class be placed in an open order for exercising. Sometimes it is enjoyable to work in a circle formation. It is even possible to carry on calisthenics while marching in a straight line. Another way of relieving possible boredom is to give each class member a folding chair and have him march about the gym carrying the chair, moving it up and down and sideward in rhythm as he marches. At intervals you can stop them and have them set up the chairs and do exercises in, on, around, and over them before resuming the march.

Methods of Exercising

So much for getting the class into formation. Now it is necessary to start exercising. There are three main methods of conducting this work: (1) By command; (2) In rhythm or cadence, and (3) At will.

1. *Command Method.* In the command method, the class is called to attention and then ordered into the starting position for the exercise. The instructor then describes the first position of the particular exercise and as the command is given the pupils respond by assuming the first position. They maintain that position while the instructor describes the next position, and so on to the finish of the exercise. The entire exercise may also be demonstrated by the instructor before the class performs it on command.

Of first importance is the procedure to be followed in giving commands. There are two types of commands: (1) The preparatory or directory command; this consists of a brief description of what the class is to do, for example, "Hands on Hips." (2) The command of execution; this is the signal for the action described in the first phase to be consummated, for example, "Place," "Move," or "Bend." This command must be delivered in a terse, snappy manner that will incite a prompt response. A brief pause always comes between the preparatory command and the command of execution, to give the class time enough to think about the command and get ready to respond to it. This method has several advantages. Since each position is held until the executory command for the next position is issued, the pupils can be scrutinized and faulty positions can be corrected before going on to the next move.

2. *Rhythm or Cadence.* In the rhythm method, the class makes the specified moves according to a rhythm or cadence set up by the instructor. The beat or count should be even so that the participant can anticipate just when the count will be given and finish each movement at that precise time. The rhythm can be established by the teacher's counting, clapping his hands, tapping on the floor with the end of a wand or by a pianist or even a record player. One popular way of keeping time is to have the students count out loud as they perform the exercise.

More organic stimulation is derived

from exercising in rhythm than by command since no time is lost between the assuming of positions in order to explain the next move. Most children—and adults too—enjoy this method more since it appeals to their inherent sense of rhythm; there is a natural desire to respond to rhythmic beat. Then too, working or exercising to music is more pleasant and stimulating.

3. *At Will.* The third method allows the students to set their own time or rhythm for exercising. The instructor teaches the exercise and then tells the class to exercise at will. They then begin to work and stop when he calls "halt."

This method is particularly good in situations where you want the pupils to go through an exercise very rapidly. If you, as the teacher, set a rapid tempo there are some in the class who will not be able to keep up due to lack of coordination, body size, and so on. By working at will, each can go at his maximum speed. Where sustained or held positions are required, the same is true. Some can maintain the position longer than others, and each can work to his own capacity. An activity such as push-ups can be effectively carried on "at will."

There is no "best" method. Frequently all three methods will be used in one lesson. Sometimes all three will be used for one exercise.

It is best if the class stands at ease rather than in a position of attention while the explanation and demonstration goes on.

Be sure that all can see the demonstration. Sometimes a teacher makes the mistake of putting the class in the starting position for an exercise to be done on the back before demonstrating. If the class is very large, it is best for the demonstrator to perform on a platform in front of the group.

Instructor's Enthusiasm

The teacher is a very important determinant in the development of proper student attitudes toward calisthenics. The students can either like it, tolerate it, or hate it, so the instructor's first job is to motivate the activity. A desire to be physically fit must be fostered; one must want to achieve if the results are to be good. The reasons for the activity should be explained. Students should know what the values are and understand that their efforts will be an investment in their personal welfare.

Motivating Devices

Some motivating devices include interspersing simple stunts and combatives with the standard calisthenics exercises; using students to lead the class; using partner exercises where two or more work together; organizing competitive contests between groups or individuals (most repetitions within a specified time, holding lever positions longest, group displaying best form for particular exercise, group most unified in action, and so on).

Voice

The instructor's voice has much to do with the manner in which the class responds. The voice should be firm, yet pleasant. A harsh, rasping voice is not conducive to winning friends for any sort of activity. Yet the voice must have firmness, a quality of command. This is necessary to make the class know that you expect to be obeyed.

Another way in which the voice can add to the success of the lesson is to adapt it to the nature of the particular movement being done. For example, if the exercise calls for a series of sideward bending movements of the trunk with a short rebound after each movement, the movement cues should be given in a light, snappy manner. If, on the other hand, a slow extended movement is required the voice should convey that feeling by saying "s-t-r-e-t-c-h." If a relaxation is to follow the stretch, the command should be given with a release of air to convey a feeling of relaxing.

Some leaders advocate a steady "One, Two, Three, Four" count to set the rhythm. However, that can become quite repetitious after a while and position cues, such as "up," "down," "bend," "left," and so forth, can be used in place of the numbers to relieve the monotony. These cues can serve another purpose as well. They help to keep the class unified since "down" or "left" means more to a child than "One" or "Two." The group tends to stay together better.

To Start

To start an exercise in rhythm, the leader either names or explains the exercise and then says, "Ready (pause) Begin: One, Two, Three, ..." The students start to move on the command "begin" and should reach the first position just as the first count is sounded. They start the second movement immediately and reach the end of it on the second count. This continues throughout the exercising.

To Stop

To stop the exercise in a way that will allow everyone to stop at the same time, a warning signal must be given. If this is not done, a large percentage of the pupils will continue for one or more moves. One way of halting the class is as follows: Give the first count of the exercise in the normal manner. Give the second count with a rising inflection of the voice and a slight increase in volume. Substitute the word "Class" for the third count and the word "Halt!" for the fourth count. Another good method is that of saying, "Class" on the first count, "Halt" on the second count, "One" on the third count, and "Two" on the last count. The same procedure is used to stop a two count exercise. One more repetition of the Two count movement is made after the command, "Class, Halt." It is done on the "One, Two."

Of course there is no need to give a signal to stop when using the command method since the performers automatically are stopped until given a command to move. In the "at will" method, the leader simply calls "Halt!" because the individuals are all in different stages of the exercise and they can't halt in unison.

Planned Periods

To keep the calisthenic period motivating for the students, each period should be well planned. If the teacher is unsure of what he is going to do, that fact is quickly sensed by the pupils and they will lose their respect and desire to work. Also, in order that maximal benefits be derived for the time spent, careful selection of exercises will have to be made. There are thousands of possible exercises. Obviously they cannot be all used. Therefore, the ones to be used will have to be selected.

Suitable Area

The area in which the youngsters are to exercise must also be considered when selecting exercises. That is, if the only place they have to work is out on a dirt playground, exercises which call for lying or sitting positions should be avoided. Also, if they have to exercise between the aisles of seats in a regular classroom, many moves are not possible. However, if this unfortunate situation is a reality, plan to make maximum use of the desks. They can be used for front leaning push-ups, modified dips, sit-ups, leg levers, and in many other ways. The teacher's and pupil's ingenuity should be exercised in planning new ways in which the desks can be used for bodily exercise.

Attire

The clothing of the children must also be considered. This involves the girls wearing dresses in mixed classes as well as getting school clothes dirty and sweaty. Of course ideally all who participate should wear gym clothes and take a shower after class, but we are further away from Utopia than to hope for those conditions in all schools.

Variety

The participants will tend to enjoy the work more if there is variety and progression in the program. The same drill taught day after day will become monotonous to anyone. A word of caution here: Too much variety will be costly in terms of time. It takes time to teach new exercises, and the lesson may become dull and drawn out. Make small changes in the drill and thus keep it moving.

When selecting the more difficult exercises, keep progression in mind. Always try to build on something that has been learned in the past.

Scope of Exercises

In choosing the exercises to be used, keep in mind the necessity of exercising

A calisthenics class for women

all areas of the body—arms, legs, trunk, abdomen, neck, chest, back, and shoulders. It might be appropriate to add, "especially the abdominal region and the upper torso" since the strength of these areas is known to be considerably under par for the majority of American youth. Both strengthening and stretching exercises should be included. Most children in the lower elementary grades are fairly supple, but they need the stretching type of exercise to keep them that way.

The physiological effect of one exercise as compared to that of another must be considered in the selection of the exercises. With other factors equal, the one possessing the most strengthening or stretching benefits should get the nod. The number to be selected will depend on the length of time to be spent in the activity. It is better to have too many on hand than too few. The class will appreciate using two or three exercises all having the same physiological value in two minutes' time rather than repeating just one exercise for that same time. With practice, the shift from one exercise to the other can be done with almost no loss of time.

PROGRAM OF INSTRUCTION

Basically, there are just a few standard types of exercises that may be performed. But, with the number of variations that may be applied to these basic exercises, the total number of different exercises is very great.

Regular Exercises

An attempt has been made to classify the regular exercises into three groups according to the type of action employed.

These groups are:

A. STRETCHING EXERCISES—primarily involve actions of stretching, bending, twisting, rotating, etc.

B. THRUSTING EXERCISES—primarily involve actions of thrusting, stepping, hopping, leaping, bouncing, etc.

C. POWER EXERCISES—primarily involve actions of great support, prolonged holding of positions, and movements calling for great strength.

Now that each category has been identified and described, several exercises from each group will be presented. Please keep in mind that only a few in each group will be explained and many more variations could be listed if the space permitted.

A. STRETCHING EXERCISES

1. *Windmill*

STARTING POSITION—standing erect, feet spread, arms extended to the side.

Count 1—bend at hips keeping knees straight and touch the left foot with the right hand.

2—return to erect starting position.

3—bend and touch right foot with the left hand.

4—return to erect starting position.

Variation—Touch floor outside of the foot.

2. *Toe Touch*

STARTING POSITION—standing erect, hands at sides, feet together.

Count 1—bend at hips keeping knees straight and touch the fingers to the toes.

2—return to starting position.

Variations—(a) Touch knees or shins rather than toes.

(b) Alternate touching knees and toes so as to make a four count exercise.

3. *Supine Windmill*

STARTING POSITION—lying on back (supine) with arms extended to side.

Count 1—cross right foot over to touch left hand.

2—return to starting position.

3—cross left foot over to touch right hand.

4—return to starting position.

4. *Hamstring Stretcher*

STARTING POSITION—squat position, knees together, hands on floor beside toes.

Count 1—straighten legs keeping hands touching floor and return.

2—return to starting position.

5. *Snap Up*

STARTING POSITION—stride stand, trunk bent forward horizontal to floor, arms obliquely overhead.

Count 1—reach hands between legs and touch floor as far back as possible.

2—return to starting position throwing arms vigorously upward.

6. *Arm Circles*

STARTING POSITION—standing with feet together, arms extended to side and palms up.

Exercise—rotate hands upward and backward to make small circles with shoulders as center.

Variation—reverse the direction, enlarge the circles.

7. *Side Bender*

STARTING POSITION—standing erect, feet spread, fingers interlaced behind head.

Count 1—bend sideward to the left, keeping the knees straight.

2—return to starting position.

3—bend sideward to the right.

4—return to starting position.

Variation—(a) Start with hands to side. As bend is made to left, raise right arm over head, stretching as far to left as possible and keeping palms downward. Repeat on other side with left arm.

(b) Touch floor outside right foot with right hand keeping knees straight alternate to left.

8. *Trunk Twister*

STARTING POSITION—stride stand, hands clasped behind head.

Count 1—rotate trunk to the left so that right elbow points forward.

2—return to starting position.

3—rotate trunk to the right so that left elbow points forward.

4—return to starting position.

Variation—Do the same, but with the trunk bent forward horizontal to the floor.

9. *Deep Knee Bends*

STARTING POSITION—standing erect, hands on hips, feet slightly spread.

Count 1—squat to point where knees are flexed 30°.

2—continue squat to point where knees are flexed 60°.

3—continue squat to point where knees are flexed 90°.

4—return to starting position.

Variation—shallow knee bends—go to 45° and return.

B. THRUSTING EXERCISES

1. *Jumping Jacks*

STARTING POSITION—standing at attention.

Count 1—jump to side straddle position raising arms sideward and upward, palms of hands facing each other.

2—return to starting position.

2. Stationary Run

STARTING POSITION—standing erect, arms bent so forearms are parallel to floor.

Exercise—begin to run slowly, speed up gradually raising knees to the height of the hips. Run at full speed raising knees forcibly, then slow down. May be done to a count with left foot hitting each time (or every other time) the count comes.

3. Imaginary Rope Jumping

STARTING POSITION—standing at attention.

Exercise—imitate rope jumping with one or two circles of rope to each jump.

4. Squat Thrusts

STARTING POSITION—standing erect, hands on hips.

Count 1—squat fully, placing hands on floor in front of feet.

2—thrust the legs back to a front leaning rest position.

3—return to count 1 position.

4—recover to starting position.

Variations—(a) Keep legs straight rather than squat.

(b) Upon thrusting legs backward bend arms so that you end up with chest just off the floor.

(c) When in front leaning rest position, add one or two push-ups.

5. Back Leg Thrusts

STARTING POSITION—front leaning rest.

Count 1—vigorously draw both legs up to squat position.

2—extend to starting position.

Variation—Keep legs straight.

6. Side Leg Thrusts

STARTING POSITION—squatting with knees spread.

Count 1—jump to stride position with legs, keeping hands on floor.

2—return to starting position.

7. Alternating Leg Thrusts

STARTING POSITION — semi - front leaning rest, with the left leg extended backwards and the right foot outside of and beside the right hand.

Count 1—change the position of the feet by extending the right leg backwards and drawing up the left leg.

2—return to starting position.

8. Knee Grab

STARTING POSITION—sitting.

Count 1—draw both knees in to chest clasping arms around legs.

2—return to starting position.

9. Squat Jumps

STARTING POSITION—squat position with left foot forward about 8 inches and fingers interlaced on top of head.

Exercise—spring upward straightening the knees and causing both feet to leave the ground. Reverse the position of the feet while in the air, moving the right foot forward and the left foot backward. Return to squat position.

C. POWER EXERCISES

1. Push-Ups

STARTING POSITION—front leaning rest.

Exercise—bend arms, touch chest to floor keeping body straight and return to starting position. May be done to a count.

Variations—(a) Perform while supported on hands and knees.

(b) Push up vigorously so that the hands may be clapped between repetitions.

2. Sit-Ups

STARTING POSITION—lying on back (supine) hand on thighs.

Count 1—raise trunk to sitting position, reach across with right hand and touch toes on left leg.

2—return to starting position.

3—repeat Count 1 touching left hand to right foot.

4—return to starting position.

Variations—(a) Slide hands just as far as the knees and recover.

(b) With hands behind head, touch elbows to knees.

(c) With hands clasped behind head, keep back straight allowing shoulders to leave floor last.

3. Leg Lifts

STARTING POSITION—supine (lying on back) with arms alongside body.

Exercise—raise legs until vertical and lower slowly to floor keeping them straight at all times.

Variations—(a) Raise legs only 6 inches off floor, spread them apart, back together again and lower.

(b) Raise left leg only, as left leg is lowered raise right leg, alternate raising and lowering.

4. V Flexor

STARTING POSITION—supine (lying on back) with hands overhead.

Count 1—raise legs and trunk together and touch toes with hands.

2—return to starting position.

Taking a few exercises from each group, the following sequence of exercises might be formulated:

The (school nickname) Conditioner

1. Side Bender

POSITION—Stride stand, hands clasped overhead, arms straight.

Exercise—Bend upper trunk from side to side stretching with arms.

2. Side Bender (variation)

POSITION—Stride stand, arms side horizontal.

Exercise—Bend trunk to right stretching left arm overhead with palms down. Alternate to left.

3. Side Bender (variation)

POSITION—Stride stand, arms side horizontal.

Exercise—Touch floor beside right foot with right hand. Knees straight. Alternate to left.

4. Wind Mill

POSITION—Same.

Exercise—Touch floor outside of right foot with left hand. Knees straight. Alternate to other side.

5. Snap Up

POSITION—Stride stand, trunk bent forward, arms obliquely overhead.

Exercise—Touch floor with hands and return to starting position throwing arms vigorously upward.

6. Knee Grab

POSITION—Sitting.

Exercise—Draw both knees in to chest clasping arms around legs.

7. V Flexor

POSITION—Supine (on back), arms side horizontal.

Exercise—Raise trunk and legs off floor at same time touching toes with hands.

8. Push-Ups

POSITION—Front leaning rest.

Exercise—Dip touching chest to floor and push up.

9. Back Leg Thrusts

POSITION—Same.

Exercise—Vigorously draw both legs up to squat position and extend.

10. *Side Leg Thrusts*

POSITION — Squat position, knees spread.
Exercise—Jump to stride position with legs, keeping hands on floor.

11. *Hamstring Stretcher*

POSITION—Squat position, knees together.
Exercise — Straighten legs, keeping hands touching floor and return.

12. *Jumping Jacks*

POSITION—Standing.
Exercise—Jump to straddle position, raising hands overhead, palms facing each other and return.

CALISTHENICS ON THE STALL BARS

Stall bars are found in many gymnasiums but used very little. They are the horizontal bars mounted parallel to each other in a vertical line along the walls on which students like to lean and hang while they watch others being active. One reason why they are used as leaning posts is that nobody knows what else to do on them.

Stall bars may be used to supplement floor calisthenics, for they have the potential to provide exercise for nearly every part of the body. Many of the floor exercises require balance while doing them, but the stall bars provide a steady reference point while exercising, thus minimizing the balance required. Also, because they occupy so little space along the sides of the gymnasium, stall bar exercising may be done while other activities are being conducted in other areas.

On the stall bars, careful attention may be given to individual needs. Persons physically handicapped or lacking proper development in certain areas may concentrate on compensatory muscle groups or weak muscle groups. Also, for athletic events requiring conditioning of specific areas, certain stall bar exercises may be valuable.

Here are a few exercises that may be performed on stall bars.

1. *Side Bender.* Stand with the right side towards the bars about an arm's length away. Place the right foot on the second or third bar from the floor and place the hands on hips. Bend sideways to the left away from the bars and return to a straight body position. Then bend to the right towards the bars and return to the starting position. After repeating this several times, turn around and place the left foot on the bars and repeat the exercise.

2. *Trunk Twister.* Stand facing the bars about an arm's length away, and grasp a bar about chest high. Release the right hand and swing the right arm sideward and backward shoulder high, twisting at the trunk to reach as far back as possible. Return the right hand to the bar and release the left hand and swing it back in the same manner. Repeat this action, alternating arms as you do it.

3. *Back Bend.* Stand facing the bars at a distance slightly less than arm's length. Place one foot on the third or fourth bar from the floor and hook the toes behind the bar above. Raise the hands over the head about shoulder width apart and bend backward as far as possible. Return to the starting position and repeat the exercise.

4. *Squat Jumper.* Facing the bars, grasp a rung about shoulder high and stand on the lower rung with both feet. Bend to a full squat position. Simultaneously, spring from the feet and pull with the arms and jump up three or four bars from the floor, ending in a squat position. Climb down to the starting position and repeat the exercise.

5. *Trunk Bender*. Stand facing away from the bars at a distance of about two feet. Raise one foot and hook the toes over the third or fourth bar from the floor. Raise the hands over the head about shoulder width apart. Swing the arms downward, bending at the hips, and touch the floor with the finger tips. Return to the starting position and repeat the exercise.

6. *Windmill*. Stand facing away from the bars at a distance of about three feet. Raise the left foot and hook the toes over the third or fourth rung from the floor. Raise both arms out to the side shoulder high. Reach downward with the right hand and touch the floor to the left of the right foot. Return to the straight body position. Reach downward with the left hand and touch the toes of the right foot. Return to the starting position and repeat. After several repetitions, perform the exercise with the right foot hooked over the bars.

7. *Heel Kick*. Hang from the top rung facing the bars. Flex the knees and try to bring the heels as close to the buttocks as you can. Return to the starting position and repeat the exercise.

8. *Sideward Leg Swing*. Hang from the top rung facing away from the bars. Swing both legs to the left and return to a straight body position. Swing both legs to the right and return to the start-ing position. Repeat several times.

9. *Knee Lifts*. Hang from the top rung facing away from the bars. Bring the knees to the chest and return to the straight body position and repeat several times.

10. *Leg Lifts*. Hang from the top rung facing away from the bars. Raise the legs parallel to the floor without bend-ing at the knees. Return to a straight body position and repeat.

11. *Sit Up-Stand Up*. Lie on your back on the floor with the knees slightly flexed and the toes hooked under the lower rung. Raise the trunk as in doing a sit-up and grasp a rung that is about head high. Pull with the arms and extend the legs, ending in a standing position facing the bars. Return by squatting to a sitting position on the floor and then reclining to the starting position.

12. *Flag*. This is a difficult strength stunt which is very challenging. Stand with the right side towards the bars about an arm's length away. With the right hand grasp a bar about two feet from the floor. With the left hand grasp a bar about as far up as you now can reach. Keeping the arms straight, pull with the top hand and push with the bottom hand, raising the feet off from the floor. Try to hold the body in a rigid balance straight out from the bars for a few seconds.

CHAPTER 3

Tumbling

TUMBLING IS A BASIC MOTOR SKILL which covers extensively the mechanics of rolling, turning, springing, and twisting. From watching children at play one can see that it is a natural activity to include in a physical education program. Besides the fun aspect it serves as a fine background for apparatus work and also as a carry-over activity for other sports. It is challenging and exciting to develop tumbling skills whether they are elementary or advanced.

Tumbling is generally done on tumbling mats in a gymnasium, but there is no reason to avoid performing stunts outdoors on a suitable area of grass or beach.

The most common size of mat is two to three inches thick, measuring 5' x 10'. This has the advantage of being easily carried by several students and yet offering ample room for tumbling. The longer mat—up to 60'—offers an unbroken span which is better for a continual series of stunts but at the same time it is somewhat more cumbersome in transporting.

Competition is held in this event with present rules calling for four routines (or trips) down the mat within a time limit of 1½ or 2 minutes depending upon the governing body making the rules.

VALUES

The specific values of tumbling activities are:

1. Tumbling develops coordination and timing.

2. Tumbling develops agility and flexibility because of the nature of the movements involved in the activity. Much bending, tucking, and twisting is required to perform the stunts well.

3. Because of the running and springing necessary in tumbling activities, strength is developed in the legs. This is somewhat unique in that most other gymnastic activities tend to neglect the legs.

4. Courage and determination are developed in some of the more daring and difficult tumbling stunts. More advanced stunts involve movements performed with the body completely in the air.

5. Learning to control the body in basic tumbling skills has great carry-over to the other sports.

6. The art of falling correctly, as learned in tumbling, is of great importance in many sports as well as normal daily activities. A relaxed rolling fall very often prevents or reduces injury

and enables a person to regain his feet quickly after a fall.

7. Because tumbling is a natural activity, it is self-motivating and provides a great deal of fun and enjoyment for its participants.

ORGANIZATION

Area and Equipment

Beginning tumbling can be taught in a very small area. However, when more advanced stunts are taught or combinations of stunts are put into routines, a run is helpful to build up momentum. In fact, in competition a 60-foot tumbling area with additional running space is required.

Tumbling is taught best with the use of mats. The mats may be put in a small area if used by a squad only or they may be put end to end in a row for mass instruction. For a large class more than one row of mats may be required. In order for the instructor to see all of the pupils and the pupils to see the demonstration a horseshoe pattern might be advantageous. A circle formation is also possible, but doesn't enable the instructor to view the whole class as well.

Teaching Methods

Perhaps one of the major pitfalls in teaching a tumbling program is to let one pupil work and have the remainder of the class stand in line and observe. Too many instructors line the entire class up at one end of the gymnasium and have them perform individually. This type of class organization leads to discontent and will kill the fun element, with consequent discipline problems.

Beginning tumbling lends itself very nicely to the mass method of teaching. Have the class line up along the length of the mats and work across the mats on the command of the instructor. After the class executes one stunt, have them do an about face and return in the opposite direction while performing the same or another stunt. You will find that the students will not only get more activity out of this type of teaching, but they will also have more fun. It is not uncommon to see the students trying to outdo each other, consequently creating a healthy atmosphere of competition. For most beginning stunts, a maximum of three people can work on a 5' x 10' mat although two is preferable. Of course more can be accommodated by using shifts of pupils lined up one behind the other.

If the number of mats is insufficient for the whole class, tumbling can also be taught by the squad method. In this method some other activity or activities is combined with tumbling and the squads are rotated during the period. Keep in mind that other gymnastic activities probably will require mats, also. As the students become more advanced, they will require more space for tumbling and will need more rest between turns. Thus the squad method might be more advantageous for advanced work than the mass method.

Balancing activities can be combined very nicely with the tumbling instruction. They both require the same equipment and are organized and conducted in much the same manner. There is some advantage to changing periodically the type of movements, and balancing and tumbling provide a good combination for this. After performing two or three rolling movements such as is found in tumbling, it might be restful to execute two or three of the stationary movements found in balancing, and so on. Also, the two activities complement one another. For example, it is helpful to be able to do a forward roll before learning the roll out ending of a head balance. Similarly, being able to perform a head balance will be helpful in learning a headspring.

Evaluation of tumbling probably is best done by use of a stunt chart. This serves to motivate the students as well. For more advanced classes, evaluation could be based upon competitive routines.

Safety

Tumbling is a relatively safe activity. However, certain safety procedures should be practiced to cut the risk of injury to a minimum:

1. Always use mats for tumbling wherever possible. A grassy area or beach could be an acceptable substitute.

2. When using more than one mat in a row one is well advised to secure them together. This will prevent the mats from slipping and leaving "holes" in the tumbling area. Similarly guard against overlapping of mats which will cause ridges upon which one may turn an ankle.

3. When placing mats, be sure to maintain adequate clearance from walls and obstructions.

4. For purposes of comfort and cleanliness always keep the tied or button side down.

5. Inspect the mats to see that there are no ripped places in them where a performer might catch his toe.

6. To make the mats last longer always carry them instead of dragging them.

7. No student should be allowed to perform a new or intricate skill without a spotter until he is capable of doing so without danger. Encourage the students to learn the spotting techniques so that they can help each other.

8. It is very important that the necessary progression be used in learning tumbling skills. No one learns to run before he can walk. By the same token, somersaults cannot be learned before the basic fundamentals can be successfully performed. Too many instructors try to push the class too rapidly. This could result in the development of bad habits as well as injury. Fundamentals cannot be stressed too heavily.

There are two main methods of spotting; with the hand and with a safety belt. For hand spotting, one man gets close to the performer to assist in doing the stunt if necessary and to act in preventing injury if the situation arises. For some stunts two spotters are desirable. A common mistake of spotters is to stay too far away. A person falls quickly and unless they can step in and catch him the spotting is useless. However, the spotter should also be cautioned about standing so close that he hampers the performer. The performer should be watched very closely while going through the stunt so that conditions leading to a fall can be seen as early as possible. Spotters are simply to break a fall and ease the person to the mat, and not necessarily hold him clear of the mat. The best position for the spotter will vary with the stunt. In general, try to figure in which part of the stunt the fall is most likely to occur or where the most help is vital and station the spotter accordingly. When spotting is particularly important, special directions will be given along with the description of the stunt.

For advanced stunts spotting is done best with a safety belt. Generally, two people are required to assist by lifting up on the belt. For stunts involving a

Spotting

twist of the body, the ropes must be crossed around the performer in the opposite direction of the way in which the twist is executed unless a twisting belt is used.

PROGRAM OF INSTRUCTION

The following stunts are recommended for learning in the approximate order in which they appear:

1. *Forward Roll.* From a squatting position place the hands on the mat about shoulder width apart. Place the chin on the chest and lean forward, pushing with the feet and bending the arms. Allow the back of the shoulders to touch the mat first as the roll is executed and continue rolling on over the back. When the shoulders touch the mat, take the hands from the mat and grasp the shins, pulling the body into a tight tuck. Roll forward in this small ball up to the feet and then straighten up to a standing position.

After learning the technique of doing a roll from a squat, try it from a standing position. More of a forward lean will be evident when going to the mat from a stand. Be sure that the weight of the body is caught by the hands and arms rather than the head or back of the shoulders.

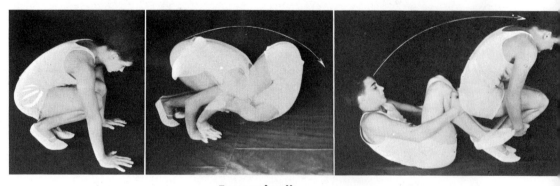

Forward roll

2. *Backward Roll.* Start from a squatting position with the hands on the mat and the knees between the arms. Lean forward slightly and then backward into the roll. Push with the hands, sit down, and start to roll onto the back. Place the hands above the shoulders with the fingers pointed back and the palms up. Keep the chin on the chest throughout the roll. Roll over the top of the head and onto the hands, keeping the knees tucked into the chest. Push with the hands and continue the roll to the feet. Finish in a squat position.

A preliminary move for this stunt is the rocker, which consists of rocking back and forth on the back with the knees in a tuck position and the chin on the chest. Keep the hands over the shoulders and rock partially on them during the rocker. Repeat this rocker motion until you have the feeling of rolling smoothly across the back, and then on one backward roll simply continue on over to the feet. This constitutes a modified backward roll.

After learning the technique of doing a roll from a squat position try it from a standing position.

3. *Shoulder Roll.* Stand at the end of the mat with the feet spread slightly. Lean forward and throw the left arm towards the mat looking between the leg, as the arm is thrown. Strike the mat at the elbow first and roll up the arm, across the shoulders and back, and end up on the feet facing sidewards. The right arm can be used to push the performer to his feet. After doing this several times, the stunt may be done from a run, simulating the fall that occurs in some games, but in a relaxed and non-injurious way.

4. *Back Extension.* This is a variation of the backward roll in which the performer momentarily passes through a

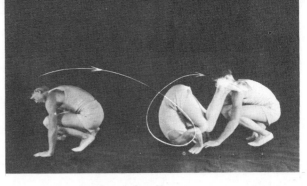

Backward roll

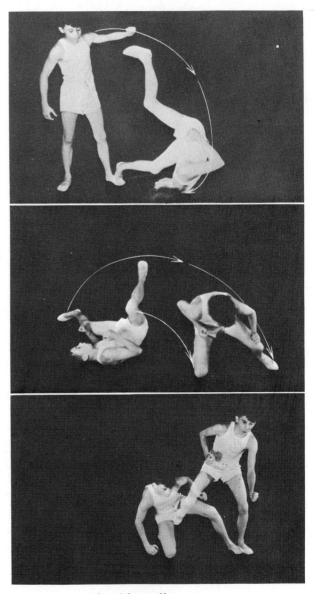

Shoulder roll

handstand position and snaps the legs down to the floor. As the performer pushes with the hands, he fully extends the arms and shoots the feet upwards to a momentary handstand. When in the handstand position, bend the knees slightly and snap the legs down from the waist. As the legs are snapped down, push with the hands so that the whole body will be completely off the mat. Finish in a standing position.

To practice the snap-down, kick up to a momentary handstand and repeat the last part of the back extension.

Back extension

5. *Cartwheel*. The cartwheel may be performed either to the left or to the right. It is here described to the left, but may be done to the right by reversing the instructions.

Start with the left side facing down the mat with the legs and arms outstretched and apart as in the spokes of a wheel. Rock to the right side by placing the body weight on the right leg and lift the left foot off the ground. Then rock back to the left by placing the body weight on the left leg. With the momentum established by this rocking motion, bend to the left side at the waist and place the left hand on the mat about 2 feet to the side of the left foot. Force the right leg overhead and simultaneously push off the mat with the left leg.

As the feet approach the handstand, place the right hand on the mat about shoulder width from the left hand. It is important here that the arms be kept straight and the head craned back so that the eyes are trained on a spot about 12 inches in front of and between the hands. At this point, the body is in a handstand with the legs held straight and apart and the back arched slightly.

As the body passes through the handstand from the side, bring the right foot down on the line established by the left foot and hand by bending to the right at the waist. The left foot will follow to the mat and one finishes facing the same direction as at the start.

In the event of difficulty in learning the cartwheel, several corrective measures can be taken. First, mark spots on the mat with chalk to show correct placement of each hand and foot. Next, try the cartwheel in the other direction; many times this will correct the difficulty. If this does not work, start the cartwheel from a squatting tuck position. From here place the left hand on the mat about one foot from the left foot. Simply jump and execute a cartwheel, keeping the feet close to the mat and placing the hands on the mat as described above. Land facing the same direction as at start. Progress by carrying the feet higher overhead until the trick is done with the body held straight.

Cartwheel

If there is trouble on the landing, practice the back end of the cartwheel separately. Kick up to a handstand and bring the right foot down close to the right hand. After the right foot strikes the ground, execute a quarter turn counterclockwise and land with the feet about shoulder width apart. When this can be accomplished successfully, try the cartwheel from the beginning.

6. *One Arm Cartwheel.* In executing the one arm cartwheel lean in the direction of the stunt and place the inside hand down and do a cartwheel without using the other arm. At first the stunt may have to be done on a small arc basis just as in learning the two arm cartwheel. As skill progresses it may be done correctly with the legs extended straight overhead and the body straight.

Roundoff

One arm cartwheel

7. *Roundoff.* The roundoff is considered an important key to tumbling, since it is used to start the majority of the backward tumbling exercises. The purpose of the roundoff is to change the forward motion, established by running, into backward motion so that backward tumbling stunts may be performed. This stunt may be executed either to the left or to the right, but for the purpose of this chapter it will be explained to the left.

Take a good run, skip on the right foot and bring the left foot forward. Place the left foot on the ground, bend forward at the waist and place the left hand on the mat about 2 feet in front of the left foot. Kick the right foot overhead followed by the left and place the right hand on the mat in front of and slightly to the left of the left hand. As the stunt progresses the hands and arms pivot in the same direction and the body turns. The fingers of both hands are pointing toward the edge of the mat. When the feet pass overhead execute a half turn. Snap the feet down from the waist and simultaneously push off the mat by extending the shoulders and flexing the wrists. Land on both feet, facing in the direction opposite from that of starting. When the feet strike the ground, bound off the balls of the feet. It is important that the eyes be trained on a spot about 6 inches in front of the hands during the entire trick. Placing chin on chest will mean loss of relative position and inability to complete the roundoff.

The roundoff should be learned from the cartwheel. The two skills are essentially the same with the exception of

Roundoff

the landing. Perform the cartwheel and instead of facing sideways on the landing, execute a quarter turn more and land on both feet simultaneously.

8. *Neckspring* (Snap-Up, Kip, Nip-Up). From a straight sitting position roll backward and place the hands on the mats behind the shoulders with the fingers pointing toward the shoulders and the thumbs by the ears. Bring the knees up to the chest keeping them apart so that they pass on each side of the head and the legs should be straight. From this position on the shoulders roll forward and at the same time (a) whip the legs forward at about a 60° angle and arch the back, and (b) push off the mat with the hands and back of the head and continue the whip of the legs

until the body lands in a squat position on the feet.

Before trying the kip in its entirety, first try a bridge position on the shoulders and feet. This will give you the feeling of lifting the hips. Then go to the bridge from the kip position on back of the shoulders using the kipping action. When this can be accomplished successfully try the neckspring as described above.

9. *Headspring.* Take a slight run, hurdle, and land on mat with both feet at the same time. Place both hands on the mat with the top of the head about 6 inches in front of the hands as though doing a headstand. Push off the feet keeping the body in a deep piked position with the legs straight. The hips are

Headspring

the near side on top of the rolled mat with the head on the far side as though going to a headstand. Move the feet close to the mat roll, keeping the body in a deep pike position until the body weight is off balance down the mat. At this point whip the feet overhead from the waist and then down to the mat in one continuous arch simultaneously pushing with the hands. Land on the feet. Once mastered from a mat roll, the stunt can be performed on a level mat as described above. The same bridging technique used in learning the neckspring is suggested in learning the headspring.

The spotter sits on the mat roll. As the performer places his hands on the rolled up mat, the spotter grasps the performer's upper arm with one hand and his shoulder with the other and assists him through the stunt.

10. *Front Handspring.* Take a good run, skip on the right foot and bring the left foot forward. Place left foot on the mat, bend forward at the waist and place both hands about 24 inches ahead of the left foot. Kick the right foot overhead followed by the left. As the feet are being carried overhead, the arms should be held straight and the eyes

carried over the head until the body weight falls off balance down the mat. Whip the legs overhead from the waist and on toward the mat in one continuous arc, simultaneously pushing with the hands. Land on the feet with the knees bent slightly depending on how high the headspring is executed. This skill is not done by kicking or pushing the feet from the knees but rather by snapping or whipping the legs out of the piked position from the waist.

The headspring should first be learned from a rolled mat and with the use of a spotter. First try the headspring from a standing position. Place the hands on

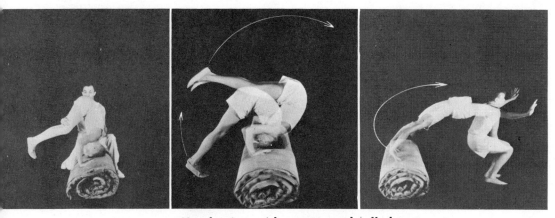

Headspring with spotter and rolled mat

Front handspring

trained on a spot about six inches in front of the hands. As the body passes through the handstand position, push off the mat with the shoulders and wrists without bending the arms. Continue on over to the feet and land with the knees flexed.

Like the headspring, the handspring should be learned with a mat roll and with the use of spotters. Start from a standing position. Place the hands on the mat in front of the rolled mat and with the aid of spotters kick up to a handstand. Arch over the rolled mat. Two spotters should assist the performer throughout this archover. Do this arch over the mat several times to establish the feeling of turning over with the arms straight, back arched, and so on. Then try the stunt with a small run and execute a front handspring over the rolled mat. The position of the spotter is to sit straddling on the rolled mat or kneeling in front of it. As the performer places his hands on the mat grasp his upper arm with one hand and place the other hand behind his shoulders. As he overbalances, assist him to a landing position on his feet.

11. *Tinsica.* Start by taking a good

run, skip on the right foot and bring the left foot forward. Place the left foot on the mat and by bending forward from the waist place the left hand about two feet in front of the left foot, simultaneously kicking the right leg overhead followed by the left and place the right hand on the mat about 6 inches in front of and about shoulder width from the left hand. The arms should be held straight and the eyes should be trained on a spot about 18 inches ahead of the hands. The legs pass overhead and the right foot lands about two feet ahead of the right hand with the left foot following and landing about 18 inches ahead

Tinsica

of the right foot. This trick should be completed facing in the same direction as starting.

The tinsica may be easily learned by using the cartwheel as a lead-up stunt. At the completion of the cartwheel as the left foot nears the mat, execute a quarter turn and come to a standing position facing down the mats. Repeat this until the quarter twist comes easily.

Forward somersault

12. *Forward Somersault*. Take a good run, skip on the left foot, bring the right foot forward, simultaneously raise both arms overhead, and land on the mat with both feet at the same time (hurdle). It is important here that the hurdle be short and fast so that the forward motion established by running may be directed upward. Throw the arms upward, forward, and downward and place the chin on the chest. Continue the circular motion with the hands by grasping and pulling at the shins, into a tuck position. The chest should be close to the knees and the heels close to the buttocks. After completing the somersault, shoot out of the tuck and land in a standing position on the mat.

The forward somersault may be easily learned by stacking mats on top of each other to a height of about three feet. Take a good run, hurdle, and execute a forward roll onto the stack of mats. Continue this action until the roll becomes easy. Progress by taking the weight off the hands until the roll can be completed without touching the hands to the mat. From here try the front somersault to a sitting position on the stack of mats. When this is completed successfully, take the mats away one at a time and try to finish standing on the feet after completing the somersault. Another method of teaching a front somersault is to provide a rolled up mat over which the performer executes a front somersault with the spotter sitting on the mat assisting throughout the stunt. The trampoline can also be used effectively to teach the fundamentals of a good forward somersault.

Still another method of learning a front somersault is with the use of a tumbling belt and two spotters. The spotters simply run alongside the performer and help him through the stunt by lifting up on the belt as the somersault is executed. A springboard trampoline can also assist the performer if spotted by this method.

When spotting this stunt without the use of a safety belt, the spotter stands at the take-off point, placing one hand beneath the performer's head or shoulders to insure a good tuck and to lift him if needed. The other hand should grab the upper arm to prevent an overspin.

13. *Tigna*. A tigna is a type of front somersault following a tinsica, in that the take-off is from one foot. The body somersaults in a semi-tuck position.

14. *Back Handspring* (Flip-flap). This is one of the more advanced tumbling stunts and should not be attempted without a spotter.

Back handspring

Start from a standing position with the feet about shoulder width apart, and the arms held straight out in front of the body. Swing the arms downward, simultaneously bend the knees and sit back as though sitting in a chair. As the body falls off balance backward, swing the arms upward overhead, simultaneously forcing the head backwards. Straighten the legs and push off the mat with the toes. As you push off with the toes, force the hips upward and make a big circle with the hands. As the hands land on the mat the body is approaching a handstand position. From this position, snap the legs down from the waist as in the snap-down and land in a standing position on the feet. It is important that you continue to force the arms over in the arc until they finally reach the mat.

When spotting with the aid of two spotters by the hand method, they should take a position on the knees or by simply standing on the mat at the side of the performer. Have the performer do a back bend and assist by supporting his body weight. When he is in the back bend position, have him keep his arms straight and force his head back so that he is looking at a spot about 12 inches in front of his hands. Carry his feet overhead so that he passes through the handstand position. Have the per-

former then come to a stand on the mat by bending down from the waist. Repeat this several times until he gets the idea of turning over. Progress by having him try the back handspring in its entirety.

To hand spot the flip-flap in its entirety, place the right hand in the small of the performer's back and use the left hand to assist him in turning over. This may be accomplished by lifting him behind the thighs with the left hand as he starts the back handspring and flipping his feet overhead. When using this method of spotting it is important to stand close to the performer since it might be impossible to support his body weight at arm's length.

A tumbling safety belt may also be used for spotting purposes in first learning this stunt. Two spotters may then assist the performer through the back-bend action as mentioned previously.

After learning the handspring from a standing position, try it from a snap-down. This involves kicking into a momentary handstand and snapping the feet down vigorously while pushing off from the fingers. This brings the performer back into a standing position with the momentum already started for a back handspring.

Back handspring from snap-down

Back somersault

15. *Back Somersault.* The standing back somersault should not be attempted without the use of a spotter. Start from a standing position with the feet about shoulder width apart and the arms hanging in a natural position at the sides. Bend the knees, drop the arms backward and jump up swinging the arms overhead as though catching a horizontal bar. Throw the head and arms backward hard, simultaneously bringing the knees up to the chest. Make a small circular motion clockwise with the arms and grasp the shins with the hands into a (tuck). While in the tuck position it is important to pull the knees to the chest hard, continually forcing the head backward. Think about kicking yourself in the chin with your knees—when you see the ground shoot out of the tuck position and land on the feet in a standing position.

Before trying the back somersault in its entirety, first attempt the jump tuck. From a standing position jump into the air and bring the knees up to the chest. As the knees strike the chest grasp the shins and hold the tuck position. It is important here to bring the knees up to the chest rather than the chest down to the knees. Shoot out of the tuck and land on the feet. Do not throw the head and arms backward when practicing this lead-up stunt as it can cause partial turnover and possible injury. A spotter may assist here by standing behind performer and simply placing a hand in his back to prevent overspring. After this jump tuck has been tried several times then try the back somersault with the use of a spotter or two.

In spotting this stunt it is suggested that two spotters be utilized, one on each side of the performer. As the performer learns the stunt, the spotters can assist by supporting the performer in the small of the back, aiding the somersault.

16. *Roundoff Back Handspring.* Take a good run and execute the roundoff as described earlier. It is important here to snap off the hands on the roundoff so that the entire body is in the air at one point. As the feet are snapped downward, they should be pulled well under the body to impart back motion. Before the feet land on the roundoff, the flip-flap should be started. The hands should come off the floor during the roundoff and be carried as though making a big circle. Keep the arms straight and continue the circle so that the hands will be forward of the center of gravity of the body when they reach the mat. Snap the legs down from the waist as in doing a snap-down and come to a stand on the mat.

Do not attempt this trick without a spotter. The method used in spotting may again be determined by the size of the performer. A small boy or girl may be successfully hand spotted. Larger individuals should be spotted with the use of safety belt and two spotters. It is important that the spotters be experienced, otherwise injury may result.

17. *Roundoff Back Somersault.* Take a good run and execute a roundoff as described earlier. It is important that the feet *are not* pulled through on the roundoff but instead kicked out backward so that the backward motion established by the roundoff may be directed upward. The arms should move off the mat directly from the roundoff and be carried upward and overhead. As the feet leave the mat, bring the knees up to the chest (tuck) and simultaneously throw the head backward. As the knees are forced up to the chest the arms complete a small circle, and grasp the shins. When one revolution is complete, shoot out of the tuck and land. The back somersault should be taken high and spun fast to give more time for the landing. In order to increase the rate of spin, think about kicking the chin with the knees as the tuck is made. While in the tuck, pull the knees up tight to the chest and force the toes overhead.

The roundoff back somersault should not be attempted without spotters. It is suggested here that the safety belt and 2 spotters be used for this stunt.

18. *Roundoff Back Handspring Back Somersault.* Take a good run and execute a roundoff, flip-flap as previously described. Snap off the hands on the roundoff and pull the feet under the body for the back handspring. The landing on the handspring is very important since it will determine the height of the back somersault. Kick back on the flip-flap, simultaneously reaching upward with the arms so that the back motion established by the roundoff and handspring will be directed upward. As the feet leave the floor, bring the knees up to the chest into a tight tuck and simultaneously throw the head back-

ward. Complete one somersault and shoot out of the tuck for the landing.

The roundoff back handspring back somersault should not be attempted without a spotter. The traveling suspension should be used when attempting this skill, or the hand belt used with two spotters running along side the performer.

Twisting Tumbling

Many tumblers may be generally classified into one of two groups: Somersaulters and Twisters. The somersaulter finds very little difficulty in doing the back somersault and even the double back somersault. This person usually tumbles with considerable height and executes a tight tuck when somersaulting. The twister, on the other hand, has difficulty in doing high somersaults and will probably find a great amount of difficulty in doing the double back somersault. This person finds twisting very easy and is able to work several twisting skills in one routine. This individual usually completes the double twist with very little difficulty and is often able to learn the two and one half twist and even the triple twist.

Some tumblers are very fortunate and possess both categories of talent. These tumblers will be able to complete the double back somersault as well as all the more difficult twisting skills.

For the purpose of continuity all twisting moves will be explained from the roundoff and flip-flap, and to the right. These moves should not be attempted until the roundoff, flip-flap, and back somersault can be completed successfully, and should be attempted only with a spotter. The twisting belt traveling suspension should be used in learning all twisting moves.

1. *Half Twisting Backward Somersault.* Start by taking a good run and execute a roundoff, flip-flap. It is important here that you kick out on the flip-flap so that the half twister is carried high. As the feet land on the back handspring carry the arms overhead and force the hips high as though doing a layout back somersault—i.e., with the body completely straight. Carry the head backward and then to the right side, simultaneously dropping the right shoulder and arm and bringing the left arm across the chest. Complete the back somersault with one half twist and land on the feet. It is important that the head and shoulders are forced over the body on landing. Failure to do this will result in under turning the somersault, causing a sit down landing.

2. *Full Twisting Backward Somersault.* As the feet land on the flip-flap carry the left arm upward and over the right shoulder, simultaneously carrying the right shoulder and elbow backward and downward. The head moves backward and to the right looking over the right shoulder. For best results the mat should be seen over the right shoulder as the twist starts and remain visible throughout the twist. The body is in a layout position with the head remaining in one spot and acting as an axis around which the body rotates. After the initial throw bring the arms into the chest to increase the rate of spin. Upon completion of one revolution force the arms away from the chest to stop the spin and land on the feet.

DOUBLES TUMBLING

Doubles tumbling consists simply of two persons executing tumbling feats together. This activity can be a great deal of fun and extremely rewarding. It does require close cooperation between the two performers, though, and it is also suggested that at least one and possibly two spotters should assist the performers. Some of the doubles tumbling stunts might include:

1. *Doubles Forward Roll.* Start with one partner lying on the mat with his feet in the air while the other stands at his head in a straddle position. They grasp each other's ankles. Then the top man dives forward into a forward roll taking the bottom man's feet down toward the mat with him. The roll brings the bottom man up onto his feet and he in turn dives forward. Then the other man is on top again so they continue in a steady roll down the mat.

Doubles forward roll

2. *Doubles Backward Roll.* Start in the same position as the doubles forward roll. The top man sits down pulling the bottom man's feet back with him. The bottom man executes a backward roll pushing up vigorously with his hands. Thus, the positions of both men are now reversed, and the stunt may be continued in a steady roll backward down the mat.

3. *Knee and Shoulder Spring.* The bottom man lies on his back with his knees raised and slightly spread. The top man approaches toward the feet and with a short run places his hands on the

bottom man's knees. As the top man performs a headspring motion the bottom man assists him by placing his hands on the shoulder blades of the top man. The top man continues over and lands on his feet just beyond the head of the bottom man.

person's buttocks rests against the lower back of the bottom man. The thrower should stop his forward lean and raise up as he feels the top man rolling off his back. Be sure to have a spotter available throughout the early learning phases of this stunt.

Back to back toss

4. *Back to Back Toss.* In this stunt one person tosses the other person over his back. Start standing back to back with the hands clasped over the shoulders. One person bends his knees and then leans forward, and proceeds to lift the other person over his back. The thrower or bottom man should be sure to dip slightly with his knees so that the top

5. *Front Flip Pitch.* Start with both performers standing facing the same direction. The flyer should bend one knee and place his shin and instep into the thrower's hands. Both performers then take a small dip in their knees and then the flyer should proceed to lift for a forward somersault with the thrower lifting hard under the top person's shin

Front flip pitch

Side leg back flip pitch

and instep. The flyer with the aid of the lift should then execute a forward somersault.

6. *Side Leg Back Flip Pitch.* The flyer places his straight leg into the thrower's hand and places his right hand on the thrower's shoulders. The thrower lifts the leg up into the air and with the aid of the other hand on the flyer's back throws him into a back flip. The flyer should keep the lifted leg taut so that the thrower will have a solid means of lifting him into the air.

7. *Back Flip Toe Pitch.* This is done by the flyer placing his hands on the thrower's shoulders and setting one foot in the thrower's hands with one foot. The flyer then straightens upward and backward into a back somersault pitch. The thrower lifts upwards into the air and throws the flyer into the somersault. Be sure to use a spotter in learning this stunt.

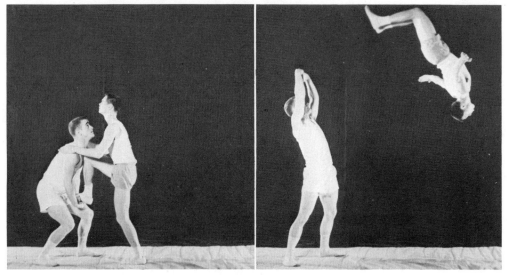

Back flip toe pitch

CHAPTER 4

Balancing

WE ALL HAVE SEEN children in the playground, front lawn or sandy beach kick upward into a momentary handstand, and each second that the balance is held becomes a moment of joy for them. It is really great fun and a matter of warm pride to accomplish a balance of some sort with a moderate degree of proficiency. Besides this fun aspect balancing does contribute a great deal to the physical development of the growing boy or girl. Very little equipment or space is required; the regular 5′ x 10′ x 2″ mat is very satisfactory for all degrees of balancing stunts. Surely an activity that offers so much return on so little investment of equipment and space should be given serious consideration in the physical education program.

Balancing as such does not lend itself to organized competition, although it plays a large part in other gymnastic competitive events, such as free exercise and parallel bars.

VALUES

The specific values of balancing activities are:

1. Balancing develops coordination and agility. The ability to maneuver the body in an upside down position and to land correctly on the feet requires a great deal of coordinated action from the entire body.

2. Strength and endurance are developed by many balancing stunts. Many balances call for holding the body in positions that depend on muscular action for support, particularly of the abdomen and shoulders. Presses often depend on strength in the arms and shoulders.

3. Balance and a sense of relocation are essential in balancing stunts and are gained through consistent practice. Poise and orientation can be developed through balancing activities.

4. Balancing develops confidence and sureness in the ability to handle the body. This is a value which all growing boys and girls should experience.

5. In executing the doubles balancing stunts a certain amount of teamwork is necessary. This value is developed through balancing as one performer depends upon another to do his part of the stunt.

6. Balancing is fun and enjoyable since it is a natural and self-motivating activity.

7. Balancing provides a chance for the small boy or girl to gain needed recognition. Very often the smaller person has an advantage in balancing over

the larger person which is different from many sports.

ORGANIZATION

Balancing needs very little equipment. Tumbling mats and space are about the only essential requirements, and even if tumbling mats are not available the activity can still be conducted if handled with close supervision and caution. Any area can be used, including a gymnasium, classroom, school corridors, and playgrounds. The important item in this respect is to provide ample space for each student.

There is very little difference in the organization and conduct of tumbling and balancing. Only the differences will be noted here and the reader is asked to refer to the preceding chapter on tumbling for the general plan.

Balancing can be taught by the mass method or by the squad method. Unlike tumbling it requires no more space for advanced stunts than for beginning stunts. Balancing work requires a lot of practice for most people, so time should be allotted for it. However, variety is also needed to maintain interest. Tumbling and a mixture of singles and doubles balancing can make a good contribution to variety. It is not necessary for singles balancing to precede doubles balancing. They both can be presented in the same lesson.

For singles balancing the students should work in pairs with one performing and the other spotting. For doubles balancing groups of three or four are best with two students performing the stunt and the other students spotting.

PROGRAM OF INSTRUCTION

The following stunts are recommended for learning in the approximate order in which they appear. The singles work will be presented first followed by the doubles balancing stunts.

Singles Balancing

1. *Squat Head Balance.* Start this stunt from a squat position with the hands on the mat and the inside of the knees resting on the elbows. From this position lean forward and place the head on the mat. Lift the toes from the mat so that the balance is on the head and hands, thus placing the performer in the squat head balance.

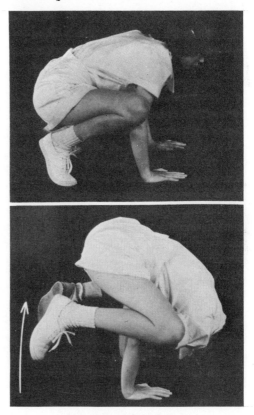

Squat head balance

2. *Squat Hand Balance.* This is similar to the squat head balance except the head does not touch the mat and the entire balance is maintained by the hands. Start from a squat position with

Squat hand balance

the arms shoulder width apart with the inside of the knees resting on the elbows. Lean forward, keeping the head off the mat, and lift the feet into the balance position. Maintain the balance by working with the arms and pressing with the fingers.

this fundamental stunt raise the feet upwards over the head. Do this slowly and the balance will be maintained more easily. Another method is to place the head and hands in the proper position on the mat and simply kick one leg up, followed with the other into the head

Head balance

3. *Head Balance*. This stunt consists of balancing on the head and hands with the feet straight overhead. One method of moving into the head balance is from the squat head balance position. After reaching the balancing point on

balance position. Be sure to maintain a triangular formation with the head and the hands and keep the back neatly arched. Also rest the head on the forward part and not the very top or back side of the head.

It is suggested that a spotter be used while learning this stunt. The best position for the spotter is to the side and slightly behind the performer. To come down from this stunt either duck the head and do a forward roll or return the legs to the mat in the same manner as they were put in position.

Spotting a head balance

4. *Forward Roll to Head Balance.* Do a forward roll and upon reaching the feet remain in a tuck position and place the hands on the mat well ahead of the feet, lean forward and reach outward with the head before placing it on the mat. Then slowly move the feet up into the balance position. Rushing into the balance out of the roll will simply cause the performer to fall forward into another roll.

5. *Head Balance—Arms Folded.* Start from a kneeling position with the arms folded in front of the chest and resting on the mats. Place the head beyond the arms and kick upward into the balance position.

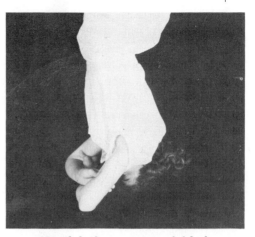

Head balance—arms folded

6. *Head and Forearm Balance.* From a kneeling position place the forearms flat on the mat with the thumbs of the hands almost touching each other. Place the head in the cup formed by the thumb and fingers of the two hands and kick upward into the head and forearm balance. This same stunt may also be done with the fingers interlaced behind the head. In either method be sure that the forearm and head form a good tripod.

Head and forearm balance

7. *Forearm Balance*. From a head and forearm balance, lift the head off the mat and maintain the balance with the forearms alone. The position may also be attained by placing the forearms on the mat and kicking upward into the balance position without the head touching the mat at all. Keep the upper arms as vertical as possible and the lower arms nearly parallel to each other.

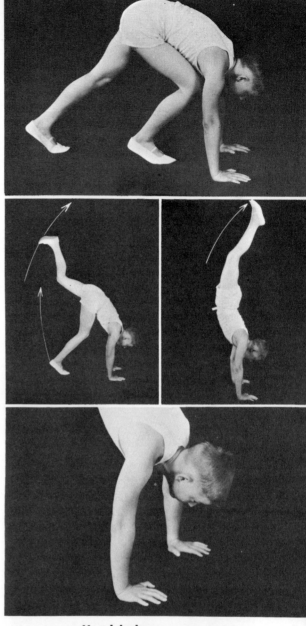

Forearm balance

8. *Backward Roll to Head Balance*. From a sitting position on the mat, roll backward as in a backward roll. When the back of the head touches the mat, place the hands beside the head and

Hand balance

Backward roll to head balance

extend the legs upward. Continue the roll to the top of the head, arch the back, and at the same time, slide the hands backward to the tripod position to stop the momentum of the moving body and to secure the head balance.

9. *Hand Balance.* This stunt consists of simply balancing oneself in an inverted position on the hands. It is a very fascinating stunt but requires a great deal of practice before final accomplishment. Once the skill has been thoroughly mastered it provides endless moments of joy and excitement.

There are several methods of learning this stunt. One of the most basic is to do it next to a flat surface such as a wall. It is advisable to use a spotter while first learning this stunt, even though support will be received from the wall. Place a mat near the wall and put the hands on the mat shoulder width apart with the fingers pointing forward, a short distance from the wall. With head up and eyes focused on the wall, kick upward until the feet rest on the wall.

Hand balance against wall

While kicking into the hand balance be sure to keep the head up to prevent the body from rolling into the wall. From this resting position push gently away from the wall with one foot so as to slowly move into a free supporting hand balance. The action on this is a back and forth motion from a free hand balance to the wall hand balance.

Another method consists of working in an open area with the use of a spotter. Execute the stunt in the same manner and let the spotter grab the legs and hold the performer in a hand balance position. Little by little the spotter can release the legs of the performer and finally a free supporting hand balance will be accomplished. It is most important that the spotter work extremely close with the performer and safely hold him in position. A safe recovery may be made from an overbalance by turning the body a quarter turn and landing on the feet. In the final hand balance remember to keep the head up (eyes looking forward slightly), back arched, and hands pointed forward with fingers gripping the floor and arms straight.

10. *Walk on Hands.* Walking on the hands is sometimes easier than holding a fixed hand balance although a controlled walk is really more difficult. After getting into a hand balance simply lean forward and before over balancing too far move one hand at a time forward a short distance. A constant lean will provide a smooth walk. Avoid taking too large a step with the hands.

11. *Head Balance to Hand Balance.* From a head balance position bring the legs downward slightly so that the body is piked a little. From this position whip the legs upward and at the same time push hard with the arms. Continue upward until the body is in a hand balance position. A spotter can be of assistance on this stunt in lifting the hips upward into the hand balance position.

12. *Bent Arm, Bent Leg Press to Hand Balance.* Start in a squatting position with the hands flat on the mat and the legs between the arms. From this position spring lightly upward in a tuck position with the hips high and the knees close to the chest. From the initial spring

continue to press upward into a handstand, straightening the legs when the hips are high enough to form an arch in the back. The arms are slowly straightened as the feet reach the hand balance position.

13. *Squat Hand Balance to Hand Balance.* This stunt is nearly the same as the preceding one except for the starting position. The performer should start from a squat hand balance. Then he should raise the hips high and slowly lift the legs upward into the hand balance. As the feet reach the peak the arms are straightened.

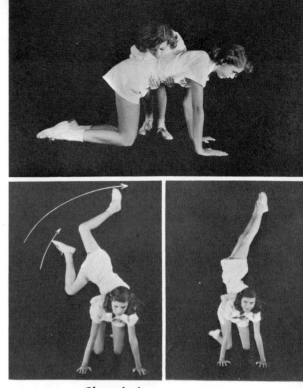

Chest balance

Two arm elbow lever

14. *Double Elbow Lever.* Start from a kneeling position with the hands on the floor so that the fingers point towards the knees. Lean forward and place the right hip on the right elbow and then the left hip on the left elbow. From this position extend the legs backward until they are straight and then raise them slightly from the mat. The body then will be supporting itself in a double elbow lever position.

Doubles Balancing

Doubles balancing is a very enjoyable activity and can readily supplement a singles balancing program. Many of the stunts are relatively easy and with a third or fourth person to assist and spot, the activity can become fun and exciting. Some of the stunts might include:

1. *Chest Balance.* Start this stunt with one partner kneeling on all fours. The other partner slides his arms under the kneeling partner's chest and places his chest on the kneeling partner's back. Then the top man kicks upward in a similar manner as backing into a head balance, and finishes in a chest balance position on his partner's back.

2. *Hold Out Facing Out (Thigh Stand).* Start this stunt by having both persons face the same direction. Then the bottom person squats down, bends forward and places his head between the top person's legs and lifts him (using the legs and not the back for lifting) into a sitting position on his shoulders.

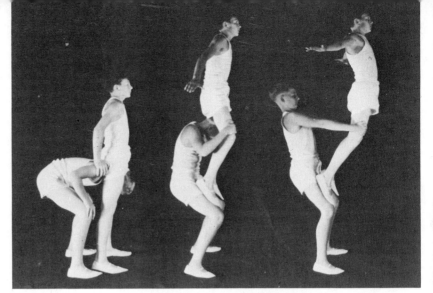

Thigh stand

The top person then places the feet on the bottom person's thighs with toes pointed downward, and the bottom man places his hands just above the top man's knees. The bottom man leans backward and removes his head from between the legs and finishes by holding the top person on his thighs with his arms straight. The top person straightens upward and forces a neat arch in the body with the arms out horizontally, head and chest erect. To dismount from this position the top man simply drops forward to his feet. The spotter should stand in front of the performers in assisting in this stunt.

3. *Hold Out Facing In.* The two partners stand facing each other. The top person circles his hands behind the bottom person's neck while the bottom one places his hands behind the top person's hips. The top man then proceeds to step upward onto the thighs of the bottom man with the toes facing outward, keeping the hips over the feet as he steps up. When a solid balance position is reached then each right arm is brought across the other's chest and a sure grip is secured on the other's wrist. From this position both men lean backward slightly and finish up in the Hold Out Facing In position. Some persons find it easier to grasp right arms

as part of the starting position and simply step up onto the bottom man's thighs and proceed to lean into the Hold Out Facing In.

4. *Knee and Shoulder Balance.* One partner is in a supine position with the hands and knees raised and the feet on the mat close to the buttocks. The top person places his hands on the knees and his shoulders in the bottom man's hands. From this position kick upward into a knee and shoulder balance. Be sure that the top person's arms are kept straight throughout this stunt, and that contact is made with the shoulders into

Knee and shoulder balance

the bottom man's hands before kicking upward into the balance. The spotter can stand by the side of the performers so as to assist in reaching the balance position.

Front swan on feet

5. *Front Swan on Feet.* One partner lies in a supine position with the legs and hands raised. The top man faces his partner and places his pelvis on the bottom man's feet with the latter's heels angling in toward the stomach and the toes outward. The men grasp each other's hands. Then the top person leans forward into an arched balance position on the feet. Hold the hands until the balance is secure and then release the grip and lift the arms gracefully to the side supported by the bottom man's feet.

6. *Back Swan on Feet.* This is similar to the Front Swan except the top man is balanced on his back. The top partner backs into the upraised feet of the bottom man and leans backward into the Back Swan on Feet. The bottom man's heels are inward and the toes pointed outward; the feet rest on the small of the upper man's back.

7. *Foot to Hand Balance.* The bottom man lies on his back with hands beside his head and the legs raised upward. The top person stands lightly on bottom man's hands and grasps the uplifted feet. The top person jumps upward slightly and pushes downward on the bottom man's feet. Simultaneously, the bottom man lifts the hands straight upward to a straight arm position. When this foot to hand position is secure the top person releases the bottom man's feet and stands up in a comfortable standing position.

8. *Two High Stand.* The partners stand facing in the same direction with the bottom man's hands resting just

Foot to hand balance

Two High stand

above his shoulders and the top man behind him, grasping the bottom man's hands as in a handshake. The top man then moves to the side of the bottom man and the bottom man squats down a little. From this position the top partner places his right foot on the bottom man's thigh and proceeds to climb upward onto the shoulders. The bottom man pulls with the arms and keeps both arms firm and strong while the top man is approaching the final position. When the top man's foot is on the far shoulder of the bottom man then the other foot is removed from the bottom man's thigh and placed on the other shoulder. The hands are still clasped and after a good balance position is obtained then the hands are released and the bottom man's hands are placed behind the top man's knees just above the calf. The top man's shins should be resting on the back side of the bottom man's head and the bottom man's hands then in effect pull downward and forward on the top man's legs. This makes for a solid two high stand. To dismount, the bottom man

lifts his right hand, and the top man grasps it and proceeds to leap forward turning slightly to his right as he leaps to the ground. Another method is to simply jump forward off the shoulders to the mat. As skill progresses the two persons may want to finish the dismount by doing forward rolls after the top man lands on the mat.

Be sure to work with one or more spotters on this stunt. The spotter should be behind the top man while he is climbing up to the shoulders and assist by pushing upward under the buttocks, and so on.

9. *Shoulder Balance on Feet.* The bottom man is in a supine position with the hands and feet raised. The top man stands behind the head and grasps the bottom man's hands and places his shoulders in the bottom man's feet. The top man then jumps upward in a tuck position and continues to press upward into the shoulder balance on the feet. Pressure is applied to the hands in order to complete the press to the balance. When the shoulder balance on the feet

Shoulder balance on feet

is secure the hands are released and the top man places his hands on the lower legs of the bottom man and continues to hold the shoulder balance on the feet. This same balance can be done in the opposite direction with the top person starting from a position behind the buttocks.

10. *Low Arm to Arm Balance.* The bottom man is in a supine position with the arms up and the legs straight out on the mat while the top man straddles the bottom man's waist and leans forward and places his upper arms in the bottom man's hands. The top person grasps the backside of the bottom man's arms; he then jumps upward into a tuck position and continues to press into a low arm to arm. This position can also be reached by kicking upward with one leg followed by the other. Keep the head

up and grasp the arms firmly for support. This stunt can also be done from knee and shoulder balance with top man transferring one arm at a time from the bottom man's knees to his arms.

A good combination is to have both men lying in a supine position, head to head, grasping each other's arms. The top man executes a back extension up to a low arm to arm balance.

11. *Low Low Hand to Hand Balance.* The bottom man is in a supine position with the arms along his sides. Bend the arms and raise the hands upward, keeping the elbows on the mat. The top man stands straddling the bottom man's head and places his hands in the bottom man's hands. The top man then kicks upward into a hand on the partner's hands. Work closely with a spotter on this stunt. Remember to allow the bottom man to

Low arm to arm

do most of the balancing by shifting the hands and arms. The top man should simply maintain a rigid position.

12. *Low Hand to Hand Balance.* The same as the low low hand to hand except that the bottom man's arms are raised straight up from the shoulders. From this position the top man kicks upward into the hand balance position.

13. *High Arm to Arm Balance.* The partners stand facing each other with arms raised and each grasps the other person's upper arm. The top man then leaps towards the bottom man and circles his legs around the bottom man's waist. He then swings down between the bottom man's legs and then back upward toward the high arm to arm position. The bottom man swings the top man up and tries to move under him so that the final part of the stunt can be done in a slightly press motion. The top mounter swings freely upward into the high arm to arm position allowing the bottom man to move in and hold him up over his head.

Pyramids

Combinations of balancing stunts can be put together to form pyramids. Because of the great number of possible combinations no attempt will be made to cover specific pyramids. Instead, general principles will be given and the readers can use their own imagination and creativity.

1. The usual shape of pyramids is either a convex curve with the peak in the center or a concave curve with a peak at each end.

2. The performers may be arranged in such formations as a line or a circle and may utilize apparatus or equipment such as parallel bars, vaulting bucks, ladders, chairs, tables, and flags.

Back extension to low arm to arm

3. For large pyramids the group may be arranged in units each of which could be a pyramid in itself. In this case the highest unit would be in the center with the lower units at the sides.

4. If the pyramids are being performed as a part of an exhibition, some attempt should be made to select and arrange the group on the basis of the sizes of the individuals. Of course, ability will be a limiting factor. For example, if a head balance is to be performed on each side of the middle unit, the appearance would be better if two individuals of the same height and build were selected.

5. If the pyramid involves building on top of one another, the stronger and heavier members of the group should be used to form the foundation.

6. Pyramids are usually formed "by the numbers." The group should be lined up in rows with the top men standing behind the bottom men. Then some sort of signal is given for each step or movement until the pyramid is complete. Another signal should be given to dismount which usually is done forward and may include a forward roll upon

Low low hand to hand

Low hand to hand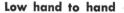

hitting the mat. The pyramid need not be held for a very long time. The instructor, upon watching the performance, can judge the amount of time which would be most effective.

7. Very often a lack of ability may be compensated by having a person held in a balance position by another person. For example, two performers may do hand balances facing each other and have their legs held in place by a third person standing between them. Also, such stunts as merely standing on a kneeling partner's back or on the backs of two people in a push-up position make suitable parts of a pyramid without needing any particular ability.

An example of a pyramid involving simple singles balancing stunts would be:

High arm to arm

squat hand balance—head balance—forearm balance—hand balance—forearm balance—head balance—squat hand balance

An example of a pyramid involving simple doubles balancing stunts would be:

knee-shoulder balance—hold out, facing out—two high balance—hold out, facing out—knee-shoulder balance

A few pictures of various pyramids are included to help stimulate the imagination of the instructor.

Pyramid

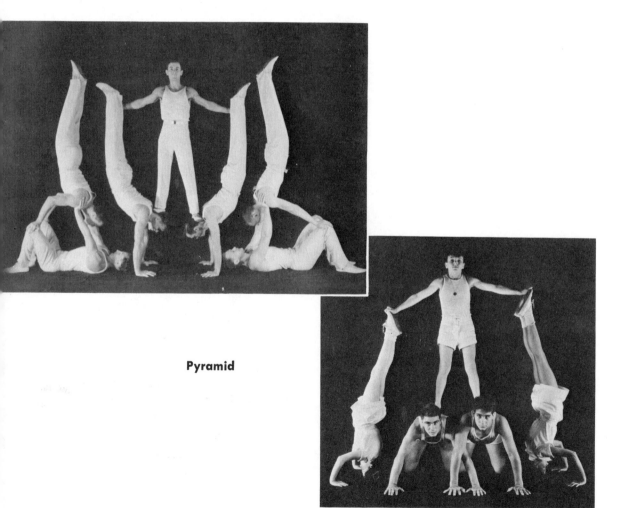

Pyramid

CHAPTER 5

Free Exercise

THE FREE EXERCISE event can be one of the most exciting and creative activities in gymnastics. The range of ideas and the scope of imagination that enhances this event is unlimited. A performer can execute stunts of great flexibility, stunts of tremendous strength, stunts of soft agility, stunts of keen tumbling and balancing and stunts of imaginative rhythm. It has been only in recent years that this event has been used to any extent in American gymnastics, but it is receiving greater enthusiasm with each ensuing year of competition.

The free exercise area is 12 meters (39.33 feet) square. The surface used in America is the floor but in Olympic Games a thin resilient pad is provided. The area is generally lined with an inch line of either paint or tape. To leave the area while performing the free exercise routine is an indication of poor planning and results in a reduction of points from the judge's score. With this in mind it is imperative that the area be properly marked as an aid to the performer.

Olympic rules governing this event call for a minimum of one minute and a maximum of one and a half minutes for the completion of the free exercise routine.

VALUES

The specific values received from working this event are:

1. The tumbling values already covered in the tumbling chapter are similar in that it develops timing, agility, and the musculature of the legs.

2. The values received from the balancing are the development of a keen sense of balance and coordination. The minute control of intricate balance positions calls for the utmost in coordination and cooperation of all the muscles in the body.

3. The strength moves executed in free exercise develop power and strength, particularly in the upper body.

4. The flexibility movements develop suppleness to its highest degree.

5. The creativity of the exercise calls for keen imagination and expression not found as readily in the other events.

ORGANIZATION

In first learning free exercise movements it is highly recommended that a tumbling pad be used. After many suc-

40940

cessful completions on the mats the stunts may be tried on the floor. The trend seems to be toward providing a special free exercise pad but lacking this, mats should be used for learning. Free exercise is different from other gymnastic activities in that it is taught in part in a class situation. The skills of tumbling and balancing that make up free exercise are taught in classes and these methods have been covered in the preceding chapters. However, when basic tumbling and balancing skills have been learned, some time can be taken from the class period to put together some combinations of stunts. A basic feeling for the event is cultivated this way and as skill progresses more difficult stunts may be introduced.

Because of the creativity, originality, and individuality that is desired in this activity, perhaps the best work can be done with individuals, particularly at the more advanced stages. However, elementary free exercise can be given by mass instruction methods. Large groups can go through elementary movements together and with practice can use such synchronized routines for exhibitional purposes. Such exercises as swinging the arms, into a front scale, into a forward roll, to a V seat, or side body roll can be used for mass work. Be sure to allow ample room between the students.

Work with the spotter in many of the intricate agility stunts. The half twisting back dive into a forward roll, valdez, mule kick into splits, and so on, are easiest learned with the help of a spotter.

PROGRAM OF INSTRUCTION

Free exercise routines generally consist of a mount or starting stunt followed by the body of the routine consisting of stunts of all types and finally a finishing stunt, often called a "dismount." For an effective opening the mount is usually explosive or dynamic in nature. The majority of the performers start with a run and execute a short tumbling routine either backwards or frontwards. If a performer isn't an effective tumbler then he may start with an equally impressive strength or balance stunt. The same effectiveness is attempted in the finishing stunt and many performers again use a running start and finish with tumbling stunts. For the middle of the routine, it is desirable to have a good representation of stunts from each category. Descriptions and learning techniques are given by categories in the following pages.

Balancing Stunts

The balancing stunts consist of any movement that has an element of stationary pose to it. Stunts such as head balance, hand balance, scales etc. all belong in this group. Each will be described separately.

1. *Front Scale (Forward)*. Scales are probably the easiest balancing moves that can be learned, but unless they are done gracefully, it is best to omit them from the routine. The easiest scale is done by starting in a standing position and then slowly leaning forward so that the upper body lowers to a position parallel to the floor and at the same time the left leg is elevated to make a straight line with the chest in that it is also parallel to the floor. The arms are held in swan position with the head up and the back arched or the left arm is kept along the side of the body and the right arm extended forward parallel to the floor. The leg is extended backward in a taut yet smooth position with the toes pointed.

Front scale

V seat

One arm elbow lever

Wide arm hand balance

2. *Side Scale.* This same type of scale can be done to the side by leaning to the right and lifting the left leg. The right arm is held close to the head and extended out to the right with left arm along the body down towards the knee. From here the performer may execute a cartwheel into a handstand, and so on.

3. *Needle Scale.* This is done by simply lifting the left leg up into the air to the side of the performer and the ankle of the lifted leg is grasped with left hand and the entire leg is pulled in as close to the body as possible.

4. *Knee Scale.* A very elementary move is to do a one knee scale from a kneeling position. Simply lift one leg back and lower the chest parallel to the floor. This is very similar to the forward scale except that the performer is resting on one knee with the shin and instep adding to the support.

5. *V Seat (Balance Seat).* This consists of merely sitting on the floor with the legs elevated and straight. Thus the body assumes a V position. The hands may be on the floor behind the performer or raised out to the side.

6. *Two Arm Elbow Lever.* See description and pictures in Chapter 4.

7. *One Arm Elbow Lever.* Similar to the two arm version, except that the weight of the body is on one elbow. Steady the balance with the free hand and then lift it from the floor, holding it straight out in a line with the legs.

8. *Hand Balance.* This is probably one of the most commonly used stunts. There are many different methods of moving into the hand balance position and some of these will be covered in the category of presses. For greater difficulty this stunt may be done with the arms spread. For complete description of a hand balance, refer to Chapter 4.

9. *Yogi Hand Balance.* This is merely another version of holding a hand balance. After complete control of the hand

balance position is reached then slowly bring the head forward between the arms and allow the hips to move in the opposite direction with the legs piking downward slightly. This awkward looking handstand has been named a Yogi handstand because of the unique position of head, hips and legs.

10. *L Seat On Hands.* From a sitting position with the hands on the floor at the side of the hips lift the legs and body upward and hold this L Seat with the hands supporting the entire body.

11. *Straddle Seat On Hands.* Sit on the floor with the legs in a straddle position. Place the hands on the floor between the legs and then lift the entire body upward supporting the weight by the hands and arms alone.

Strength Balance Moves

These stunts are generally called "presses," and as implied they consist of balance movements with an element of strength or power required.

1. *Squat Press to Head Balance.* From a squat balance with the knees resting on the elbows, place the head on the floor and slowly raise the hips and legs upward into a head balance.

2. *Bent Arm Straight Leg Press to Head Balance.* From a kneeling position place the head on the floor and lift the hips upward keeping the toes on the floor with the legs straight. From this pike position slowly lift the legs upward into a head balance position.

3. *Bent Arm Press to Hand Balance.* From a squat position on the floor press upward into a hand balance. The legs at the start of this stunt may be either between the arms or resting on the elbows. In pressing to the hand balance position be sure to move the hips upward and forward to a position above

Straddle seat

Bent arm press to hand balance

Bent arm straight leg press to hand balance

Ball through arms to hand balance

the hands and then continue the press by bringing the legs in a tuck position on up to a full hand balance. A spotter can assist by holding the performer's hips and steadying them as the stunt is tried.

4. *Bent Arm Straight Leg Press to Hand Balance.* From a pike position on the floor with the arms bent and the hips high and toes resting on the floor press upward with the legs straight into a handstand position. Be sure to move the hips forward and upward to a position above the hands and then the remainder of the press becomes easier.

5. *Ball Through Arms to Hand Balance.* Start from a sitting position on the floor with the hands at the side of the body. Elevate the body with the hands and then ball the knees into the chest and on through the arms. Continue the movement through and on up into the hand balance. This stunt can also be done supporting the weight on the fingers of the hands.

6. *Tiger Press.* From a forearm balance position lean forward, shifting the weight towards the hands and then press upward into a hand balance position. This is a stunt that calls for great strength in the arms. A spotter can assist by grasping the performer's ankles and lifting upward.

7. *Arched Roll to Hand Balance or Head Balance.* Start by lying prone on the floor with the hands at the sides of the body near the hips. Lift the chest upward and from this position roll downward and forward onto the chest and up toward the hand balance. Remember to rock forward onto the hands and with the momentum of the roll push hard with the arms and finish in the hand balance or the more intermediate position of the head balance.

Agility Stunts

This area of free exercise is one in which an imaginative person can create many new and different stunts of agility that fit in well with a free exercise routine. These stunts generally arouse much interest and appreciation in participants as well as spectators.

The following are but a few of the many stunts that can be done in this group:

1. *Straight Fall to Prone Position.* This generally follows a tinsica or handspring. The momentum is simply continued and the performer falls downward toward the floor with one leg elevated. The body is caught with the arms and by flexing slowly and smoothly the chest continues downward to the finish position.

2. *Backward Fall with Half Turn to Chest.* From a standing position fall backward and immediately execute a half turn to the left and continue to fall toward the floor with the front of the body facing the direction of the fall. Catch the weight of the body with the arms and flex them softly with the fall. Finish with the left foot and the hands and chest resting on the floor and the right leg raised upward. This is more often done after a starting stunt such as a back somersault.

3. *Straddle Leap.* Leap into the air, raising legs parallel to the floor, and touch the ankles with the hands. This stunt is generally done prior to executing a front flip, or a leap to a hand balance position, and so on.

4. *Flying Leap.* Take off from one leg and leap into the air and execute a half turn of the body and land on the other foot in a balance position with the arms out to the side with the upper body parallel to the floor, very similar to a Forward Scale.

Backward fall with half turn to chest

5. *Pinwheel.* Start from a squat position with the hands on the floor in front of the body with the left leg stretched out to the left side of the body. Bring the left leg forward and round in front of the body lifting one arm at a time as the leg passes under them. Continue the swing of the left leg behind and under the right leg which is continually flexed and finish up in the starting position. This stunt is generally done two or three times and thus has a pinwheel action. Be sure to keep the left leg straight with the toes pointed throughout the stunt.

6. *Pinwheels to Elbow Lever.* Execute two or three pinwheels and near the end of the final one extend the right leg back with the left and drop both hips onto the elbows and finish in a double elbow lever.

7. *Neckspring with Half Twist.* Execute a high neckspring and immediately after the whip of the legs has started execute a fast half twist. After the twist land on both hands with the feet extended to a front resting position. It is highly important to do the spring high in order to complete a clean half twist.

8. *Front Support with Full Turn.* From a front support position with the arms straight and legs extended backward push hard with the arms and at the same time bring one leg up slightly. Support the body on the flexed leg and execute a full turn of the body and land back on the hands again in a front support position.

9. *Shoot Through to L Seat.* From a front support position with the arms straight and legs extended backward push with the hands slightly after a flexion of the hips downward and then shoot the legs through the arms and finish in an L sitting position supporting the body with the arms.

Pinwheel

Shoot through to L seat

Straight leg roll

Valdez

Back roll to straddle stand

Half twisting back dive to roll

right leg the performer executes a quick back bend motion into a hand balance position. It is imperative that a spotter be used while first learning this stunt.

14. *Half Twisting Back Dive to Roll.* Start from a standing position and leap backward and execute a half turn of the body landing on the hands and continue into a forward roll. It is important to lift the legs and hips upward as the stunt is executed and then the forward roll can be done smoothly. A spotter can be of assistance by lifting up under the performer's hips during the first part of the stunt.

10. *Straight Leg Roll.* This consists of executing a forward roll with the legs straight throughout the stunt. It is important to push hard with the hands as the body completes the roll since this helps the performer to roll up to his feet. Remember to keep the head and shoulders forward during the latter part of this stunt.

11. *Back Roll to Straddle.* Execute a backward roll and when the weight is on the hands spread the legs and continue the roll finishing in a straddle stand position.

12. *Headspring to Straddle Seat on Floor.* Execute a high headspring and immediately after the whip action has started, pike the body strongly and spread the legs and land on the floor in a straddle sitting position. Try this stunt several times on a mat before attempting it on the floor.

13. *Valdez.* Start from a sitting position with the left hand placed on the floor behind the back with the fingers pointed away from the body. Keep the right leg straight with the left leg bent and the left foot near the buttocks. Raise the right hand over the head. With a push off the left foot, a throw backward of the right arm and an upswing of the

Double around to L seat

Splits

15. *Double Around to L Seat.* Start in a front rest position. Flex the hips slightly and then bring the legs around the left arm. Lift the hand as the legs pass under it and quickly drop it to the floor so as to catch the body in an L seat position.

Flexibility Stunts

There are several stunts that are grouped in the flexibility category, and these stunts demand a great deal of looseness and suppleness of the joints and muscles. Many of these stunts are not particularly difficult but they do require time and constant practice to accomplish them.

1. *Splits.* This simply consists of standing with one leg ahead of the other and slowly lowering the body downward into a splits position. By placing the hands on the floor on each side of the body a small cushioning effect is produced. The same type of splits can be done sidewards with the legs out to the side and the upper body forward parallel to the floor.

2. *Backbend from Kneeling Position.* From a kneeling position lean backward until the head touches the floor. The arms may be held along the side of the body for additional support or straight outward for an effective backbend motion.

3. *Head to Knees.* Start in a standing position and then bend forward and place the hands behind the thighs and continue bending forward until the head touches the knees or shins. Constant practice will produce the flexibility necessary for this stunt.

CHAPTER 6

Trampolining

TRAMPOLIN is a Spanish word meaning "diving board" and refers to just that in any of the Latin American countries, Spain and Mexico. In Germany the word refers to a springboard or to juggling. Very little has been written about the beginning and the progress of the sport of trampolining. A French circus acrobat of the middle ages, whose name, "du Trampoline," may also be legendary, is said to have started first working on the springboard and leaping board, and then visualized the possibility of doing tumbling stunts on the safety net suspended under the flying trapeze acts. He reduced the size of this net and then performed on it with a unique repertoire of flips, twists and turns. This net was gradually reduced to approximately its present size.

After this start the trampoline grew in popularity and soon each circus had its bounding bed act.

After this initiation many YMCA directors, physical education teachers and gymnastic coaches adopted the main idea of the bounding bed construction and built them for their gymnasia and camps.

After some years of research and development, the "Nissen Trampoline" was patented and manufactured in quantity in 1939. At the present time several companies manufacture trampolines and different sized models have been introduced.

Trampoline

Trampoline from underneath

The trampoline consists of a sturdily constructed table-high frame approximately 9' x 15', within which is attached, by means of elastic cord or metal springs, a heavy canvas or woven webbing sheet which serves as a performing surface. The junior size trampoline stands about 2' high and is about 5½' x 9'. The giant sized trampoline has a frame that is approximately 10' x 17'.

The trampoline has been accepted as an official event in gymnastic meets by the NCAA and NAAU governing bodies. It has proven to be very popular with spectators as well as participants. Competitive rules vary but at present can be summed up as follows: Competition is composed of two sequences or routines separated by a 20 second rest period. Each routine includes a maximum of eight or ten contacts or bounces with the counting to start at the completion of the first stunt. The number of contacts is determined by the governing body making the rules.

VALUES

The specific values of working the trampoline are:

1. More than in any other activity, trampolining develops a sense of relocation.

2. The many movements made while in the air display the development of timing, rhythm and coordination.

3. Trampolining requires and develops confidence and self reliance.

4. The trampoline, along with tumbling, excels among gymnastic activities in developing the legs.

5. Trampolining is one of the most enjoyed activities in gymnastics. Perhaps the inherent desire to bounce or the ease with which the bouncing is done is responsible for the fun found in participating in this activity. Enjoyment motivates intensive participation.

ORGANIZATION

Area and Equipment

The trampoline can be used in a class without occupying too much space. Just a few feet of space on each side of the trampoline is all that is needed although the ceiling should be of sufficient height to allow free bouncing. Depending somewhat on the age of the class, the minimum ceiling height should probably be about 15'. The area immediately surrounding the trampoline should be clear of obstacles that would hurt a person falling off the device. If sufficient mats are available an additional safety precaution would be to put mats on the floor around the trampoline.

If more than one trampoline is available for the class, it would be advisable to put them a few feet apart and parallel to one another. This would concentrate the activity in one area. Wherever the activity is located in the gymnasium, it should be within clear view of the teacher. Sometimes it is helpful to have a platform between two trampolines the same height as the trampolines. This would allow very close supervision of a class involving just two trampolines.

Teaching Methods

If the trampoline instruction is to be profitable, there should be no more than six or ten students to each trampoline. Any more than ten will prevent the students from getting enough time during the class period to practice the stunts. If the class is too large for the number of trampolines, other gymnastic activities could be carried on elsewhere. This would probably be done best by dividing the class into squads and rotating the squads during the period.

One of the problems facing the instructor is organizing for best use of the trampoline by the class. Too often, an instructor will allow one student to monopolize this equipment while the other students only stand and watch. The watchers lose interest and are apt to engage in "horseplay." The following suggestions may aid in efficient organization:

1. Make it clear that those standing around the trampoline are spotters and have an important job to perform.

2. Plan your schedule beforehand to insure that each student will have some time to practice on the equipment. A system of rotating the students from spotter to performer back to spotter is highly advisable.

3. Practice one stunt at a time. It is much wiser to have all students in your group learn at least one stunt than have part of the group learn several while the remainder have learned nothing. A good rule of thumb is to allow no more than thirty seconds per man per turn. In this way you are sure to give everyone a chance to perform.

Demonstrations should progress from the simple stunts to the more difficult. Sufficient time should be spent on each stunt before the student is allowed to progress to the next. However, this may become a problem because some students may have more ability than others, and consequently will progress faster. You probably will find it advisable to rearrange the group so that you are teaching groups of equal ability rather than groups of unequal ability. This not only makes teaching easier, but creates a better learning situation for your students.

As an instructor, undoubtedly you have some degree of proficiency in trampoline stunts. This should enable you to perform your demonstrations easily, but remember that because it is easy for you to demonstrate, it is not as easy for the beginning student to follow the demonstration. Accordingly, you should demonstrate the stunt several times until you are sure the students have grasped what you are trying to show them. While this may take a bit more time initially, in the long run it is quicker. After you have demonstrated a stunt, be sure to ask the group if they understand what they are going to try to do. Once the group appears to have grasped the point of the demonstration, give them the opportunity to practice the stunt. Don't start another demonstration—you will only confuse them.

Since trampolining is a self-testing activity, it is probably best evaluated by some form of stunt chart. Attractive, well-kept charts are good for motivating the students, also. If checking individual stunts is too time-consuming, well-spaced routines might be used to check achievement and progress. For more advanced classes, it would be possible to judge the students in competitive routines, taking into account form and continuity as well as difficulty.

Safety

One precaution should be noted in trampolining and that is safety. This does not mean trampolining is dangerous. If properly used, the trampoline is not. Instructors should remember that the dangerous element in trampolining is the illusion of foolproofness that is created by the soft springy bed. Students may easily get the feeling that they can't get hurt. This can lead to taking unnecessary chances and result in injury. Showing off can be dangerous. If, however, you closely supervise trampoline activities, these stunts can be learned with little or no danger.

Good equipment properly maintained is basic to all other safety precautions. Trampolines are sturdy, well constructed pieces of equipment, built to last for many years, but like all other types of equipment, misuse can damage them. Therefore, it is important that you, as instructor, take precaution to insure they are used properly. The following points should prove to be of value:

1. The trampoline should never be left unsupervised. When you have finished with it, it should be folded up and stored away. Too often trampolines have been damaged and people hurt because the trampoline was left out and was used by inexperienced students who thought it would be fun to bounce on.

2. Never allow students to wear street shoes when using the trampoline.

3. "Horseplay" should never be allowed on a trampoline—it is not designed for such use.

4. Inspect the trampoline before and after it has been used. This not only protects the trampoline from further damage, but is an excellent means of preventing accidents.

As to actually conducting the class for trampolining there are some basic safety hints which should be adhered to:

1. There should be a minimum of two spotters, one at each end of the trampoline. If more are available space them around the trampoline.

2. Safety pads should be provided for the metal frame of the trampoline.

3. The progressive order of learning the stunts should be closely adhered to.

4. Learn early how to "stop" the bounce by flexing the knees immediately upon landing on the canvas. This will prevent an uncontrolled bounce off the bed.

5. To prevent possible injury come to a complete stop before dismounting and place your hands on the frame to support yourself as you crawl off.

6. Remember that in bouncing, control is more important than height.

7. To prevent losing control the trampolinist should bounce for short periods of time such as less than a minute and best about 30 seconds.

8. Horseplay should not be tolerated.

9. Not more than one student should bounce until after they have become quite proficient at single trampolining.

10. A hand or overhead safety belt should be used in learning the more difficult stunts.

PROGRAM OF INSTRUCTION

Before beginning discussion of the stunts it is important to understand the basic trampoline activity of bouncing. Bouncing on the canvas of the trampoline is similar to bouncing on a spring board or diving board. The feet must be kept about a foot and a half apart

Bouncing

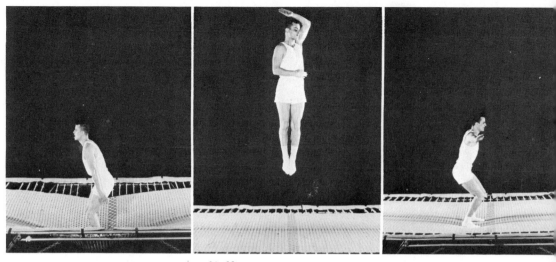

Half pirouette

while on the bed. A good measurement is to keep the feet apart about shoulder width distance. The legs must be kept together while in the air. The knees must be bent slightly when contacting the canvas and the legs straightened while in the air. One must lift with the arms on the upward bounce of the body and drop the arms when coming down in preparation for the next upward bounce. The body must be kept straight, the head up and eyes forward.

Some preliminary bounces and lead-up stunts before actually attempting the trampoline stunts are as follows:

1. *Half Pirouette.* Bounce straight up into the air and execute a half turn, twist or pirouette so that the body is facing the opposite direction upon landing. In twisting pull one hand across the waist and the other hand behind the head.

2. *Full Pirouette.* Same as the half pirouette except complete a full turn.

3. *Tuck Bounce.* Bounce straight up and when off the bed draw the knees up to the chest and grasp the shins with the hands. This places the body in a

tuck or ball position. On the way down release the tuck and land in a standing position.

4. *Pike Bounce.* Bounce straight up and while in the air lift the legs so they

Tuck bounce

Pike bounce

64

Seat drop

the legs contact the canvas simultaneously. The trunk is slightly inclined backward from the vertical. Hands are flat on the bed six to eight inches in back of and to the side of the hips, with the fingers pointed toward the feet with the arms slightly bent. Return to the feet.

6. *Front Drop.* Land on the bed in a prone position. Extend the arms forward with the elbows extended sideward and

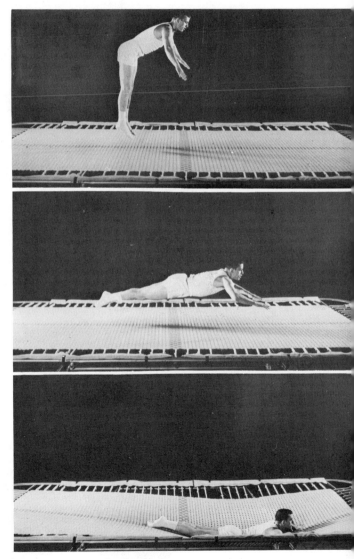

Front drop

are parallel to the bed. While in this position the hands should touch the ankles. Remember to keep the legs straight throughout the performance of this stunt. On the way down snap the legs down and land in a standing position.

These few preliminary bounces and lead-up tricks serve as "feelers" and will aid tremendously in acquiring confidence and courage for the more advanced stunts.

5. *Seat Drop.* Land on the bed in a sitting position with the legs fully extended forward so the entire back of

the palms of the hands downward. The following contact points should land simultaneously: palms, forearms, abdomen, and thighs. Try this first from a hands and knees position and then from an upright standing position.

7. *Back Drop.* Land on the bed in supine position with the legs straight and vertically inclined. Place the hands on either the thighs or free of the legs but near them. Keep the chin on the chest. Try the first few by leaning back-

position. In first learning this stunt keep the bounce extremely low and don't allow the back to arch too much upon landing on the knees. An arched back has a tendency to snap the performer forward which results in a strain of the back muscles.

9. *Half Twist to Back Drop.* Begin as if going into a front drop and upon leaving the bed throw one arm across the waist and turn the head in the same direction thus twisting the body into a

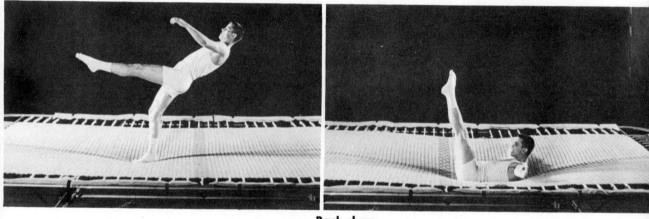

Back drop

wards from a standing position and lift one leg up to help tip the body into the back drop position.

8. *Knee Drop.* Land on the bed in a kneeling position with the contact point being the knees, shins and instep. Be sure to keep the body directly above the knees when landing in the knee drop

half turn. Proceed to land in a back drop position.

10. *Half Twist to Front Drop.* Start as if going into a back drop and upon leaving the bed execute a half twist of the body by pulling one shoulder back and piking the body slightly. Look into the twist and when facing the bed ex-

Knee drop

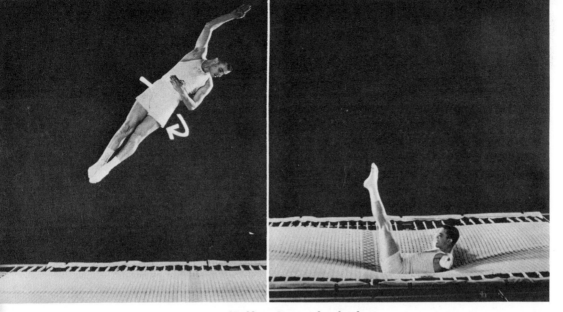

Half twist to back drop

tend the legs and prepare for the front drop position.

11. *Junior Routines.* About this stage of your learning program you are ready to try to put a few of these basic stunts into small junior size routines. Some of these might be:

a. Seat Drop—Knee Drop—Seat Drop—Feet
b. Front Drop—Feet—Seat Drop—Feet—Front Drop
c. Front Drop—Knee Drop—Seat Drop—Knee Drop—Front Drop

d. Knee Drop Half Twist—Seat Drop
e. Front Drop—Seat Drop—Front Drop—Feet
f. Front Drop Half Twist—Seat Drop
g. Seat Drop—Back Drop—Feet
h. Front Drop Half Twist—Back Drop
i. Back Drop Half Twist—Front Drop

12. *Back Drop to Front Drop.* In first trying this stunt it is suggested to do a back drop and shoot forward to a hands and knees position. This should be tried several times before attempting the final stunt. It is important to obtain a solid

Half twist to front drop

landing in the back drop position with the legs up at an open pike position. From this position a kip or kick is obtained by extending the legs forcefully forward and upward. Upon leaving the bed the shoulders are rolled forward and the legs are tucked under the body. When the body has rolled over to an almost parallel position above the bed then extend the legs backward and place the arms forward and sideward in preparation for the front drop position.

13. *Front Drop to Back Drop.* From a front drop landing push with the forearms and thrust the body backward by tucking the legs into the chest and forcing the chest backwards. Continue on over until in back drop position and then open the tuck and land on the back.

14. *Swivel Hips.* From a seat drop landing lift the arms over the head and extend the legs downward. Twist the hips a half turn and swing the legs under the body in a pendulum fashion After the half twist is finished flex the hips into a seat drop position and land on the seat. For the first few times do a seat drop and execute a half twist and land on the feet and then continue on to another seat drop. Do this several times until the "feel" of the stunt is acquired and then attempt the entire swivel hips.

15. *Seat Full Twist to Seat.* This stunt is first done from a sitting position on the bed. The body is rotated in the direction of the twist and the hands are placed on the bed near the hips in the direction of the twist. The hands support the body and the complete full twist is executed and the seat drop position is again assumed. This should be done several times to acquire the feel of the full twist. The seat drop full twist to seat drop is done from a standing position then drop to a seat drop landing in

Swivel hips

a slightly leaning backward position. Extend the body and go into the twist by thrusting one arm across the waist with the other arm behind the hips. Keep the body extended throughout the twist and upon completing the twist pike the body and land in a seat drop position.

16. *Front Dive to Back Drop.* This consists of diving over to a back drop landing. Remember to keep your eyes on the bed until about two feet above it and then duck the head and land on the shoulders. Keep the hips forward so that a good back drop landing is obtained.

17. *Half Turntable.* After landing in a front drop position turn in one direction by pushing hard with the arms in the opposite direction of this turn. Upon bouncing off the bed tuck the knees into the chest, keep the head low and look into the direction of the turn. Upon finishing the half turntable open the body and land in a front drop position.

18. *Back Drop Pullover.* This stunt is a back drop or hip landing and a pull backwards into a back pullover to the feet. In first learning this stunt, try several backward rolls from a squat position. Place the hands over the shoulder on the first few tries to assist in pushing the body over the head. After the backward roll has been done satisfactorily several times, then the same roll is done from a standing position. The technique here is simply to sit and roll on over into a backward roll. With the standing start the body generally obtains a small bounce upon landing on the hips prior to the backward roll. After a few of these have been tried then try with a couple of bounces. Land on the hips in a slightly tucked position. From this position pull back under the thighs with the hands and continue on over to the feet. Gradually increase the height of

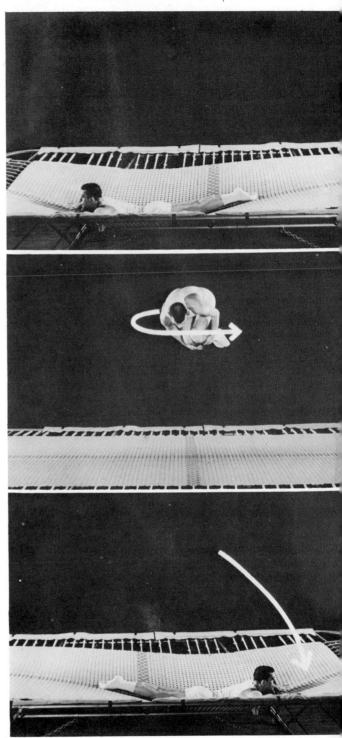

Half turntable

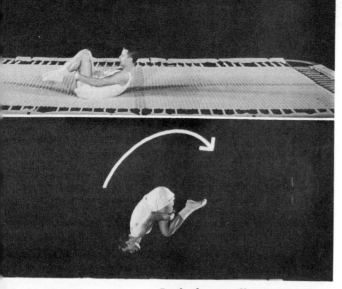

Back drop pullover

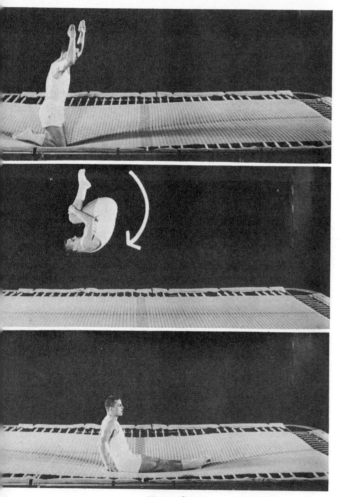

Knee front somersault

the bounce as the stunt becomes perfected.

This stunt has several variations, including Back Pullover to a Front Drop, and Back Pullover to a Back Drop Landing.

19. *Cradle.* This stunt is started from a back drop landing and as the body bounces forward as if rolling over to a front drop position one arm is thrust across the waist and the head is turned into the direction of the arm thrust and a half twist is executed. The stunt continues into a backdrop landing.

20. *Front Somersault.* It is suggested that the front somersault be learned first from the knees. Before this, though, several forward rolls should be done to acquire the feeling for the somersault. Then try it from a knee drop landing. Upon landing on the knees lift the arms up and forward and at the same time look into the direction of the somersault. At first the stunt should be done only to the back which acclimates the performer with the feel of the somersault. After this has been done several times then try the front somersault to a seat drop landing. Finally the entire stunt is done. Remember in executing the front somersault from the knees to the feet to lift the arms up and forward as the legs drive down into the bed. Look into the direction of the flip and then grasp the shins with the hands and pull the knees into the chest into a tight tuck. Hold on to the tuck until the somersault is almost completed and then extend the legs downward towards the bed leaving the arms up and forward of the chest. Next do the front somersault from the feet. This may be accompanied by a spotter bouncing along with the performer or by using a safety belt.

21. *Back somersault.* On the take-off raise the chest into the air and press

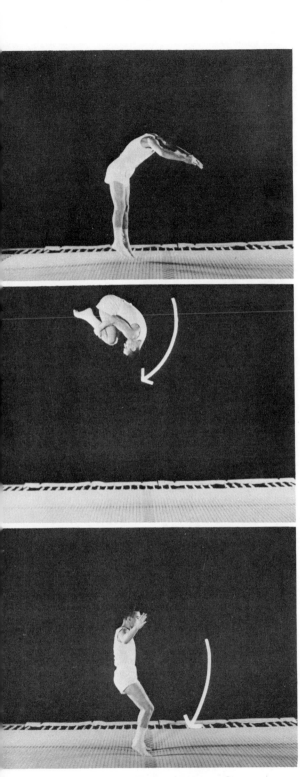

Hand spotting

Safety belt spotting

Front somersault

Back somersault

away from the bed with the legs and at the same time lift the arms up past the chest and tilt the head backwards to look into the back somersault. After leaving the bed bring the knees up to the hands and the hands should grasp the shins and pull the body into a tight tuck. Continue the back somersault and when the somersault is near completion release the tuck and extend the legs downwards for the landing.

22. *Barani.* A barani is a front somersault in a pike position with a half twist. The best way to learn this seems to be by doing a knee bounce and going into a handstand and executing a half twist and continuing over to a knee drop position again. This is somewhat like a roundoff from the knees. After doing this several times, try to finish on the feet. Remember in doing this stunt to get a strong lift of the hips at the start and thrust the body into a good forward momentum movement before executing the half twist. Be sure that the legs describe an arc over the head and not to the sides as is often the case with beginners. Next try the roundoff from the knees to the knees without touching the hands, and the stunt will then be a knee barani. Do several of these and finally try the barani from the knees to the feet and then attempt the final stunt, which is the barani from the feet to the feet.

There are several other ways that the barani can be learned and these will be mentioned briefly.

One method is to try a front somersault with a half twist using the twisting belt. By doing the front somersault in pike position and then excuting a sharp half twist a barani can be learned. Since this stunt is somewhat "blind" the twisting belt is essential for safety.

Another method is that devised by LaDue and Norman and is outlined

Knee barani touching hands

completely in their book.* It entails a front somersault from the knee to a layout back drop landing. After several of these have been tried then do a quarter turn on the last part of the stunt and

---

* F. LaDue, and J. Norman, *This is Trampolining* (Cedar Rapids, Iowa: The Nissen Company, 1955).

Knee barani

Barani

land on the side of the body. Next try the same thing except turn half way and land in a front drop position. This is the crucial spot of the entire stunt. Do many of these and be sure that a good front drop landing is obtained before moving on to the next step. The next step involves the same type somersault except that the knees are brought in toward the chest on the finish and a knee landing is obtained. This then is the same as a knee barani. After many successful knee baranis have been completed try the stunt to the feet. The same learning progression may be tried from the feet to the feet and in this way the barani is learned.

23. *Three Quarter Back Somersault to Front Drop.* This consists of doing a back somersault for three quarters of the way over and then landing in a front drop. In trying this stunt for the first time land on the hands and knees instead of the stomach. This will prevent unnecessary jarring or straining of the back due to improper landing. On the take-off the arms are lifted straight up and the hips seem to slide forward and upward. The head goes back to look into

the stunt. Try to spot the stunt and open up flat for the front drop landing.

24. *Front One and One Quarter Somersault to Front Drop.* Try a few front somersaults that are turned a little too far and land on the feet leaning forward. After acquiring the feeling of going a little too far on a front somersault then try the complete stunt. Hold on to the tuck a little beyond the opening point for a front somersault and extend the legs backward and thrust the arms forward in preparation for the front drop landing. It is suggested that this stunt be learned with the use of an overhead safety belt. For more difficulty a half twist just before finishing will put the performer in a back drop position.

25. *Back One and One Quarter Somersault to Seat Drop.* Execute a back somersault and hold on to the tuck a little beyond the point of opening up to the feet. Upon reaching this point extend the legs forward and place the hands behind the hips and keep the shoulders forward. Land in a seat drop position.

26. *Back One and One Quarter Somersault to a Back Pullover.* Complete a

Front 1¼ to front drop

back somersault and continue toward a seat drop position but land on the hips with the body in a semi-tuck position. From this landing continue into a back pullover to the feet. Pull with the hands under the thighs upon landing on the hips as this aids in completing the pullover.

27. *Kaboom.* In doing this stunt land in an extended backdrop position with the legs raised about a foot above the bed. Immediately upon landing on the back, drive the heels forcefully into the bed keeping the legs straight. The heels bounding into the bed serve to flip the body backward into a flip. Upon leaving the bed the knees are brought into the chest and the kaboom is completed.

28. *Cody.* This stunt is a back somersault executed from a front drop position. Upon landing on the stomach get a feeling of sinking low into the bed. The knees should be bent slightly. Push hard with the arms and force the chest up and back. Upon leaving the bed grasp the shins and pull the body backward into a tight tuck. Complete the somersault to the feet. This can be done easier after a ¾ back somersault to the stomach.

29. *Twisting Mechanics for the Back Twisting Series.* The basic mechanics of the full twisting, double twisting and triple twisting somersaults are very sim-

ilar. The take-off for all three twists resembles the take-off for a back somersault layout. As the number of twists is increased (full, double, triple) the somersault should become more stalled. On the take-off the arms should lift straight over the head, a little further apart than shoulder width. There should be very little bend at the elbows. The straight arm position will give more force and momentum to the twist when the arms are finally folded into the body. When the arms are extended all the way overhead before a twist to the left, the right arm should be pushed out to the side and swept across the abdomen up towards the chest. The performer should think of keeping his elbow straight at the beginning of the sweep and as the arm reaches across the left side of the body it should be folded into the chest. The tighter the arm is drawn to the chest the more force the twist will have. Very little force is required for the full twisting back somersault.

Simultaneous with the right arm sweep is the movement of the left arm, which is bent slightly and forced backward and down in the direction of the twist. As the twist progresses the left hand and arm are folded into a position directly in front of the chest. As mentioned above a tight wrap-up of both arms will increase the speed of the twist.

Upon completion of the twist the arms are thrust forcefully from the body which serves as a means of stopping the twisting action.

It is highly recommended that the Pond-Medart Twisting Belt be used in learning the twisting back somersault.

Remember while twisting to keep the body in a firm position with toes pointed, legs straight, stomach taut, and so on. A sloppy, loose appearance is undesir-

able for its own sake as well as for its interference with the performance.

Dismounts

The students may want to try a couple of easy dismounts and so the following are suggested:

1. *Side Dismount.* Land in a back drop position near the side of the trampoline over which the dismount is to be executed. Upon landing on the back extend the legs over the frame of the trampoline and at the same time pull with one hand by grasping the edge of the bed. Turn the body toward the frame as it passes over to the ground. If necessary use the hands to aid in clearing the frame.

2. *End Dismount.* Stand on the end frame and drop to a back drop and then shoot the body feet first over the frame to a standing position on the ground. The hands may grab the edge of the bed and by pulling with the arms aid the performer in clearing the frame to the ground. Remember to keep the feet low in passing over the frame.

Full twisting back somersault

CHAPTER 7

Side and Long Horse

FRIEDRICH JAHN is credited with inventing the side horse with pommels in the early 1800's. This apparatus lends itself both to vaulting and to the support type of work. The vaulting phase is somewhat easier and less dependent upon strength and as a result generally precedes the support work.

The side horse is a leather covered cylindrical body of about 14" diameter and 5' 10" length. It is supported above the ground by two legs attached to a wide base. The horse has two pommels or handles near the center about 16-17" apart. The height of the horse may be adjusted from approximately 3' to 5' although the regulation height for competitive purposes is 4' to the top of the pommels.

The long horse is the same as the side horse with the pommels removed; as the name implies, it is used along its length, instead of across. In competition, the height from the floor to the top of the horse is 4' 3".

Organized competition for men is held in long horse vaulting and side horse support work. In the former the gymnast executes the same vault twice or two different vaults with the better of the two scores counting. This event differs from the others in that the judge works only on form, the difficulty having been predetermined from a table of difficulties. The side horse support work competition consists of a series of successive stunts performed to make a smooth routine, trying not to touch the floor nor the horse with the body.

VALUES

The specific values of working the side horse are:

1. Side horse work develops strength

The side horse

SIDE AND LONG HORSE | 77

in the upper part of the body, particularly the arms and shoulders.

2. A person needs agility for the vaulting stunts and thus develops it from this type of work.

3. Coordination, rhythm, balance, and a sense of timing are all factors which are developed particularly by the support work. The constant shift in weight and cutting action of the legs in a limited space make these values especially important.

4. The side horse provides an outlet for activity for many kinds of handicapped people. Since most of the stunts involve action of the upper body, a person with an impediment in the legs can safely work on this piece of apparatus and receive much joy and recognition for it. Records show that men who have been paralyzed from the hips down have been champions.

ORGANIZATION

Area and Equipment

The side horse itself occupies very little space in the gymnasium. Usually two 5' x 10' mats are sufficient to cover the area under the horse with one on each side. However, when vaulting, more mats may be desired at the landing area to cover more space and give added thickness. Of course, room for a short run must be provided when vaulting. When using the horse as a long horse even more room must be provided for running.

Teaching Methods

Only one person may work a side horse at one time. Most schools will not have more than two side horses so the activity does not lend itself to the mass method of instruction very well. However, most stunts, particularly the vaults, do not take much time to perform so that large squads or small classes could be kept busy at one piece of equipment without undue waiting. A vaulting buck, which is a short side horse without pommels, can be used for vaulting and many of the support stunts and is very helpful as a lead-up to the side horse itself.

Since only one person can work the side horse at one time, it is very easy to supervise this activity. Thus, the squad method of instruction fits in nicely. The side horse can be one teaching station of a gymnastic unit with the squads rotating during the period.

A good method of supervising the activity is to have the students line up and then the instructor can demonstrate the stunt. Following this the first student in line performs the stunt with the instructor spotting. After a man performs a stunt, he spots for the next one in line. In this way the instructor is free from spotting and can make corrections when necessary. Side horse work is probably best evaluated by means of a stunt chart, although actual competitive routines could be used in advanced classes.

Spotting

Safety

Support work requires very little spotting in the beginning stages since missing a stunt very seldom means falling from the apparatus. However, close spotting is necessary for the vaulting stunts where it is very easy to catch a foot on the horse, causing a fall. The following are some general safety hints to consider when working the side horse:

1. In vaulting exercises set the side horse as low as possible at first and gradually increase its height.

2. Be sure to post a spotter on the far side of the horse and near enough to prevent serious falls by the performer.

3. In the same manner place a spotter at the near side of the horse to assist and help the performer.

4. Learn the proper technique of taking off from both feet before attempting even the fundamental vaults.

5. Be sure to learn the technique of pushing downward with the hands in passing over the horse on the vaults.

6. It is advisable to have a double thickness of mats on the landing side of the horse.

7. Always work in a progressive manner in learning the stunts. Start with the easier vaults and support stunts and progress toward the more difficult as skill is acquired.

PROGRAM OF INSTRUCTION

Side horse work may be divided into two categories, one being the vaulting activity and the other the support activity. Vaulting will be treated prior to the support work although the two activities are sufficiently different in nature so that one is not dependent upon the other. The stunts as listed under each category are arranged in a progressive order of learning.

Vaulting Work on the Side Horse

Before attempting the vaulting stunts it is exceedingly important for the performer to learn the art of taking off into the vault. A lead-up for this may be by

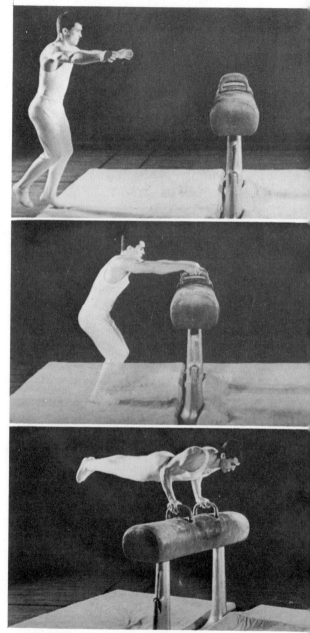

The approach and take-off

running to the horse and taking off from both feet and reaching for the pommels with the hands. Bounce off the feet, leap into the air and grasp the pommels with the hands, flexing the arms only slightly and let the feet ride upward behind the body. Do not pass over the horse but instead return to the same side of the horse from where the run started. This warm-up stunt will acquaint the performer with such principles of vaulting as: proper running approach, correct hurdle, and the take-off using both feet. After this has been done a few times the student is ready for the first series of vaulting stunts. A very gradual progression would be for each performer first to jump onto the horse in each vault position, hold it a moment and then continue off. When the idea of the vault is gained, it may be done first with a walk approach, then a jogging approach and finally a run. However, many teachers find that such a gradual progression for each stunt is not necessary particularly with the first few vaults.

Before introducing the various vaults to the students it is advisable to point out the nomenclature of the apparatus in respect to the three parts of the horse: neck, saddle and croup. As the gymnast faces the horse, the end toward his left is the neck, the saddle is the middle section between the pommels, and the croup is the end to the right. Thus when the instructor wants a flank vault over the croup the students will know that they should do a flank vault to the right.

The first four vaults may be done either to the right or left, and it is recommended that the performer learn to do the vault both ways.

1. *Front Vault.* Upon taking off, grasp the pommels with the hands, turn toward the horse and lift the legs to the left passing them over the top of the horse toward the other side. The front

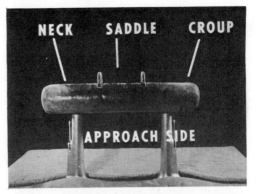

Parts of side horse

Front vault

Flank vault

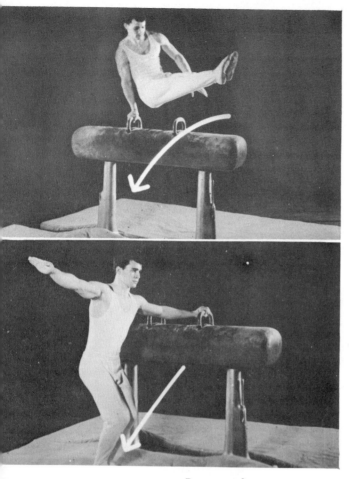

Rear vault

3. *Rear Vault.* Upon taking off, grasp the pommels with the hands and lift the legs to the left. Turn the body so that the back side passes over the horse in a sitting position. Release the left hand first and then the right in passing over the horse. After dropping with the right hand grasp the pommel with the left hand to steady the landing on the far side of the horse. Finish facing in the direction of the neck with the left side of the body nearest the horse.

4. *Screw Vault.* Approach the horse grasping the pommels with the left hand in regular grip and the right hand in reverse grip (back of the right hand facing the left hand). Upon taking off for the vault turn the right side of the body toward the horse and release the left hand. Continue the motion over the horse with the right side and then the back side of the body facing the horse. Land in a standing position facing the right end of the horse with the right hand remaining on the pommel for support.

5. *Squat Stand Leap.* Upon taking off, bend the knees and land in the saddle in a squat position with the hands on the pommels. From this position leap forward by removing the hands from the

of the body should face the horse throughout the stunt and an attempt should be made to force an arch in the body while passing over the top of the horse. As the body passes over the horse and starts towards the mat drop the left hand first, hold on with the right and proceed to land on the mats with the right side of the body closer to the horse.

2. *Flank Vault.* On taking off extend the body to the left and pass it over the horse with the flank side of the body closest to the horse. Land on the mat on the other side of the horse with the back toward the horse.

Wolf vault

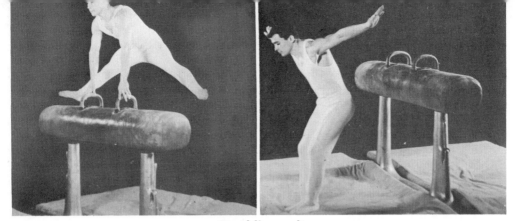

Straddle vault

pommels, lifting the arms and pushing off with the feet. Land in a standing position on the mats.

6. *Squat Vault.* On the take-off reach with the hands for the pommels and as the body passes over the saddle with the knees in a squat position push downward with the arms. Land on the other side of the horse upon completion of the squat vault.

7. *Wolf Vault.* Upon taking off, grasp the pommels and pass one leg in a tuck position between the pommels with the other leg over the end of the horse in a straight and extended position. Upon passing over the horse bring both legs together and land on the mat with the back towards the horse.

8. *Straddle Stand—Jump Dismount.* Jump into a straddle stand on the side

horse with the feet on the outside of the pommels. Lift the arms and jump forward off the horse and land on the mat on the other side of the horse.

9. *Straddle Vault.* Upon taking off, place the hands on the pommels and push downwards forcefully. Release the hands as the legs pass over the horse in a straddle position. Be sure to keep the head and chest up as the vault is executed. After passing over the horse bring the legs together and land on the mats with the back towards the horse.

10. *Thief Vault.* This vault is begun with a take-off from one foot. Run at the horse and at a distance of about 3-4 feet from the horse lift one leg up and thrust it forward between the pommels and immediately bring the other leg up adjacent to the lead leg so both feet pass

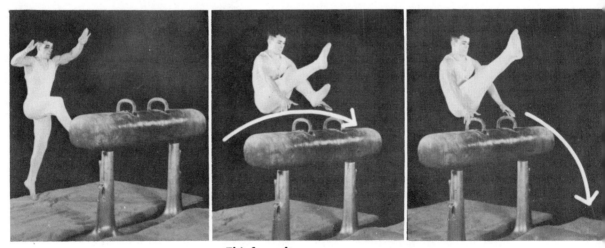

Thief vault

over the horse ahead of the body. As the hips pass over the horse grasp the pommels momentarily with the hands and continue the vault by pushing downward sending the body to the mats as the feet come down.

11. *Rear Vault with Half Twist.* Just after passing over the horse in a right rear vault position push the pommel with the right hand and turn inward towards the horse. Complete a half turn of the body and land on the mats facing the opposite direction from which it faced as the body passed over the horse. A mass drill for this stunt consists of having all the students stand facing the same direction with the right hand by their side as if grasping an imaginary pommel. Explain that all of them should feel as if they have just passed over the side horse in a rear vault position. Then they all should push with the right hand and execute a half turn in the direction of the right hand. This will give them the feel of the half twist to the right. Do this several times prior to actually attempting the stunt on the horse itself.

12. *Stoop Vault.* Upon taking off from both feet grasp the pommel with both hands and lift the legs and hips high. Then snap both legs downward between the pommels in a straight leg position. Continue the stoop and land on the mats on the other side of the horse. A practice drill for this is to stand on the horse between the pommels and kick into a momentary handstand with the hands on the pommels. As soon as the feet are up in the air snap them down through the arms into the stoop dismount.

13. *Neckspring from Knee Stand.* This stunt is done from a kneeling position in the saddle with the hands on the pommels. With a firm grip on the pommels the performer lifts his hips into the air and tucks the head back under so that

Neckspring from knee stand

the back of the neck rests on the saddle. The body should be in a pike position with the legs extended backward, and the hips forward beyond the horse. Lean in the direction of the hips and then whip the legs over toward the mats and

Neckspring

push with the hands and continue the neckspring to the feet. Land in a standing position on the mat on the far side of the horse. Spotters can be particularly effective in helping the performer by grasping his arms and assisting him through the neckspring. Continue to hold on to the performer's arms even after he lands on the mat for the first few times. This will prevent overflipping which would cause a fall on the face.

14. *Neckspring.* This is done in a similar manner as the neckspring from a kneeling position except it is done from a run. After the take-off the performer grasps the pommels and leaps into the air with the hips high. He then ducks his head and places the back of the neck in the saddle. Allow the body to continue on over the horse in a pike position; and when it reaches the point where the hips are past the horse and the body feels as if it is off-balance, whip the legs sharply over toward the mats. At the same time push hard with the hands and land in a standing position.

15. *Headspring.* Same as the neckspring except the top of the head is placed in the saddle instead of the neck. It is important to emphasize the delaying of the whip action of the legs until the hips are well past the horse.

16. *Handspring.* Same as the headspring except the head does not touch the saddle and the weight is supported by the arms in a flexed position.

Long Horse Vaulting

Long Horse vaulting is an exciting event in that a performer runs at the horse at a moderate speed, lands on a springy beat board, sails through the air over the entire length of the horse, dropping onto the hands and then continues on into vaults of various types such as stoop, straddle, hecht, or handspring.

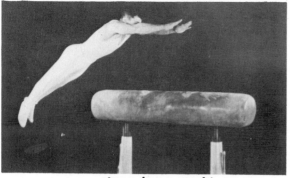

Long horse vaulting

To prepare for long horse vaulting simply remove the pommels, turn the horse lengthwise, obtain a beat board for take-off and the event is ready for action. The more recently used beat board is one which Olympic teams have been using and is called a Reuther system board. This board, built in Germany, has more spring, and makes the long horse vaulting a more exciting and easier activity. As mentioned, the vaulting is done from the beat board over the entire length of the horse. Some of the vaults that can be done and techniques of performing them will be discussed, but before this a few words should be stated regarding the proper take-off from the beat board.

Tips on Proper Take-Off from Beat Board. One of the most important phases of long horse vaulting is the proper take-off from the beat board. This takes courage, timing, and considerable practice. First of all the performer places himself at a good distance from the horse and beat board, the exact spot being determined with practice and repetition. From this position the run should start with a couple of trotting steps and as the horse is approached, should become a fast and confident run. The gaze includes beat board and horse, and surroundings, rather than only the beat board. As the board is approached, take off from one foot into a hurdle and then bring the other foot up and proceed to land on both feet. Be sure to land on the part of the beat board which will provide the maximum amount of spring. Land strongly on the board with the body more in an upright position than a forward leaning position. Remember that the run will provide the forward force but it is up to the performer to make sure he obtains a maximum spring upwards from the board. Many beginners have a tendency of simply diving over the horse with no thought of obtaining a beautiful lift or flight throughout the vault. Try one of the fundamental vaults such as straddle vault many times while trying to cultivate style and ease of performance. Proper take-off from the board cannot be overstressed. Remember to hit the board solidly, and take off with the thought of obtaining height and loft and not just skimming over the top of the horse. Also try to swing the feet high into the air before executing the particular vault in mind. The landing should also be practiced diligently since this provides the final impression and an unsure landing can detract considerably from an otherwise fine vault. Try to land solidly in one spot and avoid if possible any additional hopping or jumping around after landing on the mat. Bend the knees to absorb the shock of hitting the mat and spread the arms forward or sideward to maintain balance. When a secure position is obtained, straighten to a position of attention.

1. *Straddle Vault.* With the take-off and landing in mind the vault itself consists of simply landing with the hands on the far end of the horse, and then straddling the legs outward and forward outside of the hands. Continue the strad-

Straddle vault

Squat vault

Rear scissors

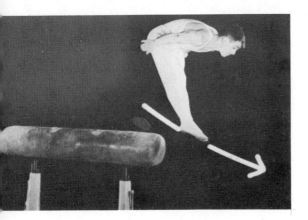

Stoop vault

dle until the horse is passed and land on the mat in a standing position. Try to elevate the legs before cutting them downward for the straddle.

2. *Squat Vault.* Similar to the Straddle Vault except that the legs are tucked into the chest and between the arms as they pass over the end of the horse.

3. *Rear Scissors* (Rear Straddle). After the two foot take-off, the hands are placed in a line parallel to the length of the horse at the far end, the right hand ahead of the left hand. The legs start off as in a straddle vault, but the right leg suddenly cuts over the horse to the left side, then the left leg over to the right side. This turns the performer around so that he is in a straddle position with the rear of the body leading the way. Of course, the vaulting body forces the hands to be released as the performer passes over the neck of the horse. Land in a standing position facing the end of the horse. Place the right hand on the end to steady the landing.

To learn the mechanics of this scissors vault, it is recommended that the stunt first be tried from a standing position on the end of the horse rather than with a running take-off from the board.

4. *Stoop Vault—from Neck.* After the take-off land on the hands on the far end of the horse with the legs in an almost hand balance position. From this position pike downward forcefully with the legs and execute a stoop through the hands. The legs are straight throughout the stunt.

5. *Hand Balance Cartwheel.* After the take-off land in the saddle with the hands together on top of the horse. Swing up into a hand balance position,

continue the swing of the feet and allow them to carry on over beyond the handstand. At this point reach out with one arm, execute a quarter turn of the body and place the reaching hand on the neck. From here allow the momentum to carry the performer into a cartwheel. Dismount off the end.

6. *Giant Cartwheel.* Similar to the Hand Balance Cartwheel except that upon taking off the beat board the performer sails into a cartwheel position by placing one hand on the saddle and from there continuing on over with the other hand so that it is placed on the end of the horse. This provides the giant cartwheel action and will carry the performer over the entire horse in a cartwheel fashion to a landing position on the mat sideways to the horse.

7. *Handspring.* Take off from the board and reach for the far end with the hands. Allow the feet to carry forcefully on upward into a hand balance position. Continue the swing of the feet upward and over the head and finish out the front handspring vault. A spotter is essential while first learning this stunt. It is also suggested that this vault be tried

Hand balance cartwheel

Handspring

at first from a standing position on top of the horse. From here simply reach downward with the hands to the end of the horse and kick the legs up into the handspring action over the end.

Support Work on the Side Horse

Support work is the activity of performing stunts while on the horse with the performer supporting himself by the arms with the hands on the pommels, neck or croup. This type of work is more difficult than the vaulting, but the participation will be as enjoyable as the vaulting phase of side horse work if a person progresses effectively.

It is important to remember a few general hints for the successful learning of support work. Some of these hints are:

1. Be sure to work from the shoulders thus supporting oneself with straight arms.

2. Learn soon to shift the weight from one arm to the other in a rhythmical manner.

3. Keep the chest up and try not to look downward too much.

4. Learn everything in small parts first and later incorporate the stunts into a presentable routine.

Many of the vaults that have been described under side horse vaulting can be used as mounts or dismounts in support work. Of course, for mounts the vault would be done from a stand and without releasing the hands, and for dismounts the vault would be done from a support position on the horse rather than a take-off from a beat board. Such vaults as front, flank, rear, squat, and straddle are usable.

Other support stunts are as follows:

1. *Single Leg Half Circle.* From a

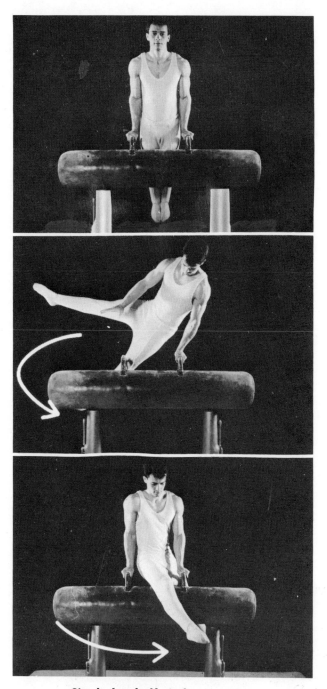

Single leg half circle

front rest position supporting the body with the arms, hands on the pommels, and the front of the body leaning on the horse, swing the right leg over the end of the horse and between the hand and the pommel. The performer then has the right leg in the saddle between the pommels on the front side of the horse and the left leg in back in original position. While the right leg is swinging over the end of the horse be sure to shift the weight of the body towards the left arm. Immediately after the right leg has passed over the right pommel, the right hand then regrasps the right pommel. Swing the right leg slightly to the left and then pass it backwards over pommel and the right end of the horse. Regrasp the right pommel with the right hand and finish up in the original starting position of a front rest support position. This stunt can be done to the left with the left leg. Most of the stunts described hereafter can be done either to the left or right, although for brevity's sake the instruction in detail for the most part will cover the right only. The understanding will be that the stunt can and should be done also to the left.

2. *Single Leg Half Circle from Rear Support Position.* Start from a rear support position with the body resting on the far side of the horse with the back of the legs against the horse. Swing the right leg backward across the right end

of the horse over the right pommel to a front support position on the other side of the horse. Return the right leg to the original starting position.

3. *Alternates from Front Support.* Start from a front support position and then swing the right leg over the right end of the horse under the hand to a position between the pommels. Then swing the left leg over the left end of the horse under the hand to a position adjacent to the right leg between the pommels in a rear support position. When the left leg reaches the rear support position then the right leg is immediately brought backward over the right end of the horse to its original position and the left leg is swung back over the left end to its original starting position.

Alternates may also be done starting from a rear support position.

4. *Single Leg Half Circle Travel.* Start from a front support position with the hands on the pommels and the arms straight. Swing the left leg over the left end and under the left hand to a position between the pommels. Swing the right leg over the right end but don't cut it under the right hand but instead

Single leg circle

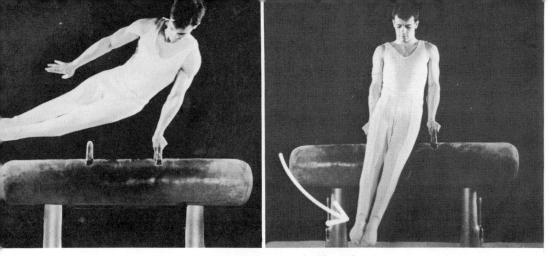

Double leg half circle

leave it to the right of the right pommel so both legs are astride the right arm (right pommel). Then swing the left leg back over the left end of the horse and shift the left hand to the right pommel. Now both hands are on the right pommel with the left hand in front of the right hand. When the left leg reaches the back side of the horse swing the right leg back over the right end and shift the right hand to the end of the horse so the body is in a front support position supported with the left hand on the pommel and the right hand on the croup (right end).

5. *Single Leg Circle.* From a front support position swing the right leg over the right end of the horse and over the pommel and continue it toward the left end of the horse and over the left pommel and then down the near side of the horse to the original starting position. Remember to shift the weight to the left when the leg is passing over the right side of the horse and then to the right as the leg continues the circle to the left side of the horse. This stunt will give the performer a great deal of practice in the skill of shifting the weight which is of great performance in side horse performance.

6. *Single Leg Reverse Circle.* From a front support position swing the left leg to the right between the right leg and

the horse, on over the right end of the horse and over the right pommel. Continue the circle of the left leg to the left and over the left pommel and left end of the horse. Finish with the left leg back at the starting front support position. The secret to execution of this stunt is a neat shifting of the weight to the left and to the right as the leg passes over the right side of the horse first and then the left side of the horse.

7. *Double Leg Half Circle.* From a front rest position swing both legs slightly to the left and then forcefully to the right over the end of the horse and over the right pommel. Finish in a rear support position with both legs between the pommels. Return by swinging both legs slightly to the left and then pass them back to the right over the right end of the horse and over the right pommel and finish in the original starting position of a front support position.

8. *Right Feint.* This movement is often used in order to obtain momentum for more advanced stunts and so should be thoroughly learned early in the learning progression. Start from a front rest support position and then shift the weight to the right arm and pass the right leg over the right end of the horse encircling the right arm. The left leg remains behind resting against the horse. Push slightly with the left knee off the horse

Right feint

a position that is parallel to the horse. The legs continue on over toward the mat and the performer lands on his feet and at the same time the left hand grasps the left pommel for a sure standing dismount.

To show how the above listed stunts fit into a routine, here is a sample: Hands on pommels, squat through to back rest; circle left leg back under left hand, right leg back under right hand, continue with both legs over neck (under left hand) to rear support, right leg back under right hand, left leg back under left hand, continue with rear dismount right.

and swing the right leg back towards original starting position and shift the weight to both arms. As mentioned this movement helps to obtain momentum for more advanced stunts such as flank circles, dismounts, and so on.

9. *Single Rear Dismount.* Start from a front support position with the hands on the left and right pommel respectively. Feint with the right leg around the right arm then swing it back across the croup and pick up the left leg and pass both legs across the neck. Both legs should pass over the neck and left pommel in

10. *Regular Scissors.* From a front support position, swing the right leg over the right end of the horse. After passing over the right end continue it down along the front side of the horse lifting the right hand off the right pommel and passing the right leg between the hand and pommel. Regrasp with the right hand and shift the weight to the right and allow the right leg to lift up above the level of the left end of the horse. The left leg follows in this same direction and when both legs are a proper distance above the horse a quick

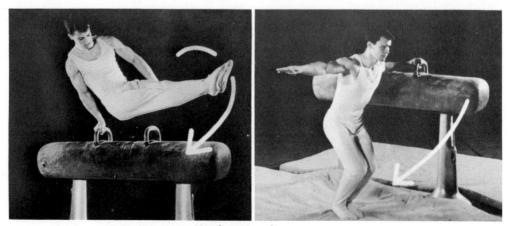

Single rear dismount

Regular scissors

scissors is executed by passing the right leg under the left leg toward the back side of the horse and the left leg passes forward above the right leg toward the front of the horse. For the best scissors movement, swing the top leg high. To finish, the left leg ends in front of the horse between the pommels; the right leg ends in back.

11. *Reverse Scissors.* Start from a scissors position in the saddle with the right leg in front and left leg in back. Swing both legs slightly forward and then back toward the right hand, shifting the weight to the left arm. Release the right hand and as the legs rise above the horse cut the left leg forward and right leg back in a scissors action. As the reverse scissors is completed and the legs swing down into the saddle regrasp the right pommel with the right hand. Finish in a scissors position in the saddle with the left leg forward and right leg back.

12. *Double Rear Dismount.* Start from a front support position as in a single rear dismount. Feint with the right leg and then swing it back over the croup. Pick up the left leg and pass both legs over the neck and continue them on in front of horse and to the right over the croup into the dismount to the mats. Throughout this stunt the weight is kept on the right arm and the hips remain close to the right arm until dropping to the mat at which time the right hand is released. A spotter can assist by standing in front of the performer and after his legs pass beyond him he can then step in towards the horse and place his hands on the performer's hips in order to help him through the last part of the stunt.

13. *Triple Rear Dismount.* Just prior to reaching the point in the double rear

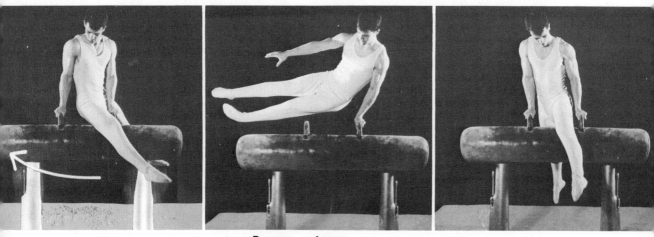

Reverse scissors

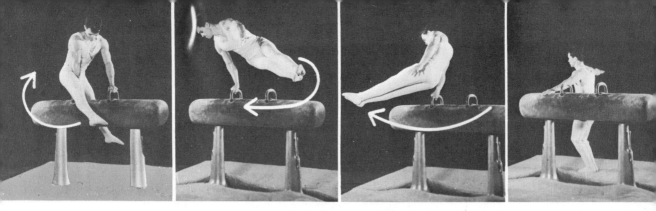

Double rear dismount

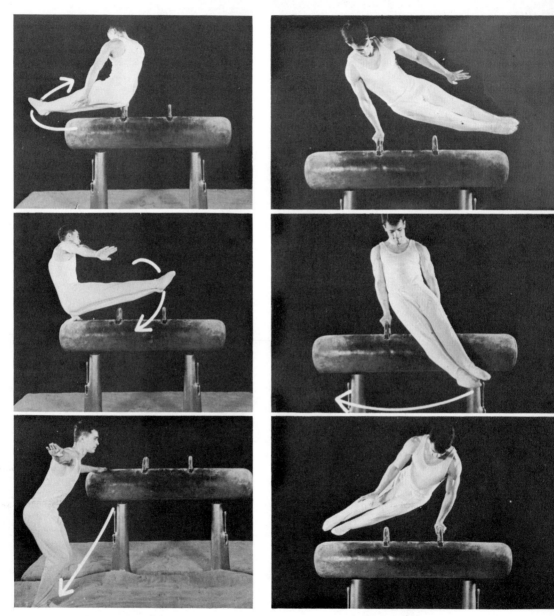

Triple rear dismount   **Flank circle**

dismount where the performer passes on over the croup to the mats, the legs continue. to circle parallel to the horse and the left arm is placed forcefully on the front side of the croup. The legs then complete the triple rear circle and pass over the pommels with the left hand supporting the body and the right hand free. After the legs and body have completed this pass, the performer drops .to the mat in a dismount stand.

14. *Flank Circle.* Start from a feint position with the right leg circling the right pommel. Then bring the right leg backwards towards a complete circle of the horse. As the right leg starts its circle, push slightly with the left knee and thus extend the left leg out in order to join the right leg in its circle. Pass both legs over the neck and continue them across the front of the horse and on to the right and over the croup. Finish in a front support position. Remember to shift the weight of the body from right to left to right, and so on, as the legs pass over the respective opposite ends of the horse. Lift the hips high in back and lower the feet and extend the hips out while circling in front. Try to keep the shoulders steady and constantly between the pommels. Also keep the arms straight throughout the stunt. After successfully completing one flank circle try doing one and half circles finishing in front. Then try two, and so on, until several can be completed.

15. *Tromlet.* After the legs pass across the front of the horse in a flank circle, shift the body over one pommel and grasp that pommel with both hands. Continue the flank circle while shifting the body on toward the end of the horse. Finish doing flank circles on the end, with one hand on a pommel and the other on the end of the horse.

16. *Double In.* Start with flank circles on the end of the horse. When the legs

Tromlet

Double in

swing toward the front after passing across the end of the horse in a flank circle, shift the weight toward the pommel arm, keeping the hips in close to the arm. Allow the legs to swing around the front of the horse and over the pommels with the body executing a half turn. Then place the free hand on the far pommel and continue with flank circles.

17. *Moore.* As the legs swing backward in a flank circle, start the Moore by turning the body inward toward the horse and reach back with the left hand and place it alongside the right. Swing the legs around the right end of the horse and then pike the body in order to pass the legs over the far pommel. After the legs clear the horse grasp the far pommel with the right hand and continue flank circles.

18. *Loop Dismount.* The loop dismount is performed on one end of the horse out of flank circles. It consists of doing a flank circle around the end of the horse while facing its length. Remember to keep the weight centered over the hands.

Routines

A small elementary routine that might be presented to the class is as follows:

Hands on pommels, squat through pommels to rear support, swing left leg back under the left hand, swing right leg back under the right hand, left leg

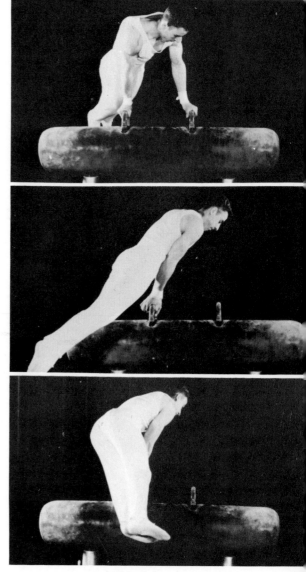

Moore

94

Loop dismount

forward into a single leg half circle travel to croup. This travel will bring the performer to a front support position on right end of horse. Then alternate half leg circles starting with left leg into a front vault dismount.

Routines of intermediate difficulty could also be worked out and rather than list a specific combination of stunts it is suggested that an exercise of one's own creation be composed from the following list of mounts, support stunts and dismounts:

MOUNTS:

1. Squat mount to half lever.

2. Double leg half circle at neck, saddle, or croup.
3. Straddle mount in saddle to rear support position.

BODY OF EXERCISE:

1. Full double leg circles right or left.
2. Scissors, regular and reverse.
3. Single leg travels, end to center or center to end.
4. Reverse single leg circles left full left or right full right.
5. Left or right hand reverse grasp and half turn.
6. Half turn forward end to center or center to end.

DISMOUNTS:

1. Double Rear or Triple Rear.
2. Flank, front, or rear dismounts with half turn.

CHAPTER 8

Horizontal Bar

FRIEDRICH JAHN introduced the horizontal bar in Germany around 1812. In his famous playground he visualized the high bar as being like the branch of a tree. Knowing how children like to play on a strong level branch he thought that they would be keenly interested in working, swinging, and performing on this high bar. His expectations were fulfilled because soon after its introduction, it was well accepted by children and adults alike. Now it is still one of the most popular gymnastic events.

The horizontal bar (often called the high bar) is a bar which is suspended parallel to the floor by two metal uprights 6 to 8 feet apart. Many bars are adjustable so that they can be lowered and raised to heights from 3 to 8 feet. The regulation NCAA high bar does not have the adjustable feature and is fixed at a height of eight feet.

In competition gymnasts are judged upon a routine which includes a series of successive stunts intended to be done without touching the mat until the dismount.

VALUES

The specific values of working the horizontal bar are:

1. The high bar develops strength in the upper part of the body, especially the arms, shoulders, chest and back muscles.

2. A good hand grip is essential to working the high bar. Constant work will strengthen the fingers and hands and insure a good grip.

3. Because of the rapid circling of the bar by the performer, a sense of re-location must be developed to reduce any dizziness caused by this action.

4. Courage and confidence in the ability to handle the body is developed from working at a considerable height with the body weight supported only by the strength of the fingers.

5. Rhythm and coordination are developed through constant practice, which in turn, reduce the demand for great strength in many stunts.

ORGANIZATION

Area and Equipment

The area required for the horizontal bar is fixed in that it uses fittings in the floor when put up. Because of this much thought should go into the placing of these fittings when being put into the floor for the first time. Proper placing will prevent interference with other activities that are likely to be conducted at the same time. Several styles of high bars are available. The wall type which is supported by cables on the one side and the wall on the other side is easily taken down and stored against the wall. It does have its drawback in that work must be performed very close to a wall. Other styles are supported on both sides by cables which may come from the ceiling or entirely from the floor. These possibly take up more floor space but are clear of building obstructions.

Mats should be used under the high bar and should extend a minimum of ten feet on either side of the bar. The area should be clear of obstructions for about 20 feet on either side of the bar, and the ceiling should be at least 15 to 17 feet high depending upon the height of the students.

Teaching Methods

Only one person should work the high bar at one time. Thus the mass method of instruction will not work very well since most schools will not have more than two high bars. Many of the beginning stunts can be tried several times if missed the first time without dismounting from the bar, but this might make the class proceed slowly. However, high bar work requires a great deal of energy and wear on the hands which calls for longer rest periods between stunts. Very often it is advisable to teach two stunts at a time to conserve strength. For example, a person might mount by means of a single knee swing-up. While he is in this position he might just as well try a single knee circle backward rather than merely swinging down from the bar. Thus, the squad method of instruction best fits this activity. Probably the high bar will be one teaching station of

a gymnastics unit with the squads rotating during the period.

The high bar can be supervised best from underneath the bar along one upright. From this position, the instructor is able to see the mistakes as they are made and give manual assistance when needed as well as closely spot the performer.

Evaluation of high bar work is easily done by means of a stunt chart. Competitive routines would also be useful in evaluating more advanced classes.

Safety

Great care should be exercised in maintaining safety on the high bar. Since the bar is fairly high off the floor and the activity involves swinging around the bar supported most of the time only by the hands, the danger of falling can be great. This is not to say that the high bar is a dangerous piece of equipment but that it requires close adherence to the safety rules. In many cases the stunts do not progress gradually so each one must be thoroughly learned before proceeding on. It is highly important that the stunts be tried in an orderly progressive manner. Stunts using basic strength are first introduced followed by stunts of agility and rhythm as the ability of the performer improves. The instructor should always be at hand to assist the performer through the learning stages of the stunts.

The following is a list of safety rules for working the high bar:

1. Check the cables and make sure they have been attached securely. This should apply also to the nuts and bolts holding the bar in place and the turnbuckles on the cables.

2. Use plenty of mats around the bar for safety and dismounting purposes.

3. Always use high bar chalk (carbonate of magnesium) on the hands.

4. Keep the bar clean of chalk and rust by using emory paper or steel wool to rub the bar.

5. Grasp the bar with the thumbs circling the bar in one direction and the fingers in the other.

6. With a few exceptions, always go around the bar in the direction in which the thumbs point.

7. Always have at least one spotter while learning new stunts to prevent slips or falls. Two spotters are preferred with one of them being the instructor.

8. In working on an adjustable bar, work low at first and gradually increase the height.

9. It is advisable to work the bar for short periods of time since the wear and friction on the hands causes blisters which often tear. When the hands are sore it is suggested that they be soaked in warm water and then rubbed with petroleum jelly.

10. It is also suggested that hand guards be worn to prevent unnecessary blistering and tearing. These hand guards may be of leather, lamp wick material or gauze.

PROGRAM OF INSTRUCTION

Two types of grips are normally used —the overhand or regular grip and the underhand or reverse grip. On the regular grip the hands circle the bar with the fingers going over the top of the bar and the backs of the hands facing the performer. In the reverse grip the hands circle under the bar with the palms of the hands facing the performer. Less commonly used is a mixed grip which consist of one hand in the overhand grip and the other hand in the underhand grip. Normally the bar is grasped with

Regular grip

Reverse grip

the hands shoulder width apart. However, for a few stunts a wider or narrower grasp may be desirable.

While first working the horizontal bar it is advisable, if possible, to lower the bar to approximately shoulder height. Later as skill progresses and as the stunts demand the bar may be elevated to the competitive height of eight feet.

Low Bar, or Learning Stunts

Stunts are listed in recommended order of learning.

1. *Front Support Mount.* Stand in front of the bar at shoulder height and grasp it with a regular grip. Jump upwards, pulling with the arms and finish in a front rest position on the bar supporting the body with the arms and with the hips resting on the bar.

2. *Back Dismount.* From a front support position swing the legs forward under the bar slightly and then swing them backwards and at the same time

Front support mount

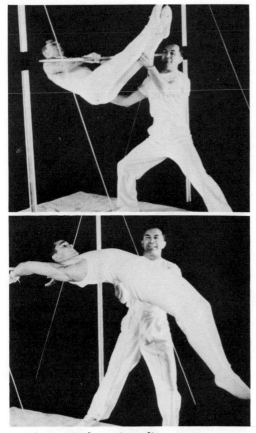

Underswing dismount

push with the hands and release the grip. Keep the body in a vertical position as you drop to the feet and flex the knees slightly upon landing.

3. *Underswing Dismount*. Grasp the bar at shoulder height in a regular grip keeping the arms straight away from the bar. Swing one leg up toward the bar and lean backwards with the upper body. Bring the other leg up promptly and shoot both feet beyond the bar in an up and outward position. Continue the sweep of the legs and pull and finally push with the hands as you release the bar. Swing the legs down to the mat and finish in a standing position.

4. *Skin the Cat*. Grip the bar in a regular grip and pull the legs up and between the arms and the bar. Continue the feet through the arms and on over as far as they will go into the skin the cat position. Return to original position by pulling the legs back up between the arms and under the bar.

5. *Single Knee Hang*. Hang under bar with overhand grip and bring one leg up in between the arms and circle the knee over bar.

Skin the cat

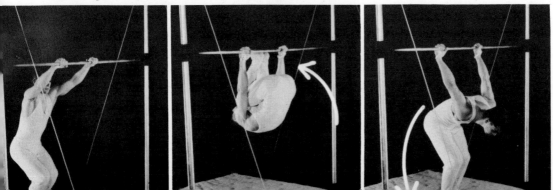

Single knee swing up

6. *Single Knee Swing Up.* Hang under the bar with one knee over the bar in a single knee hang position. The knee may be between the arms or on the outside of the arms. Swing the free leg forward and downward. Pull with the arms and allow the body to swing up to a support position on top of the bar. After this has been learned from the hanging position it may be tried from a swing with the knees being placed into the position at the front end of swing.

7. *Single Knee Circle Backward.* From a single knee support position on top of the bar swing the free leg backwards and push the body up slightly away from the bars and continue the swing of the leg downward and under the bar. Hook the back of the knee to the bar. Lean backward with the head and shoulders throughout the circle and near the finish of the stunt, pull strongly with the arms and end on top of the bar again.

8. *Single Knee Circle Forward.* Same as the backward circle but only in the forward direction. Be sure the hands are in a reverse grip position. Push up and away from the bar at the beginning and lead with the head as the circle is tried.

9. *Crotch Circle (Pinwheel).* Sit sideways on the bar with the legs straddling it and the hands grasping the bar in front of the body. From this position lean to the right and circle around the bar in a pinwheel manner. Stretch the

Single knee circle backward

Single knee circle forward

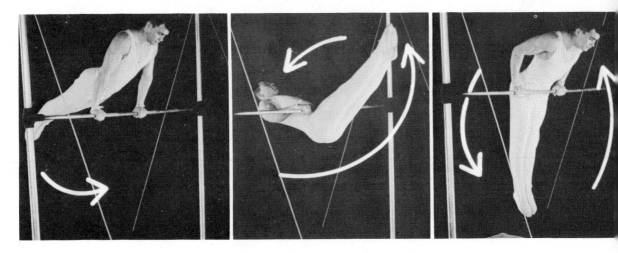

Back hip circle

body out as the circle starts and pull with the arms and flex the body slightly during the last part of the circle in order to complete the pinwheel to a sitting position again.

10. *Belly Grind.* Stand facing the bar and grasp it in a regular grip. Pull the chest into the bar and kick the legs up and over the top of the bar. Continue to pull with the arms and finish in a front support position.

11. *Back Hip Circle.* Start from a front support position. Flex the hips slightly and then extend the legs backwards away from the bar slightly. Then allow the legs to swing back toward the bar and as the thighs strike the bar, pike the body and continue the legs under

and around to the other side. Pull with the arms and complete the circle of the body around the bar. Finish in a front support position again.

12. *Double Leg Circle Backward.* Start from a sitting position on the bar with the hands gripping the bar close to the hips with a regular grip. Raise the body slightly. Shift the hips backwards, catching the bar at the knees and start to swing down and under the bar. Hold tightly with the hands and keep the knees flexed and continue the double leg circle backwards. When the hips pass the uprights and start the last half of the circle pull strongly with the arms and try to thrust the hips over the top of the bar. Near the completion of

Double leg circle backward

the stunt, shift the wrists to a support position so the hands are on top of the bar to give added support. Finish in the starting position of sitting on top of the bar.

13. *Hock Swing Dismount.* Hang by the knees and swing back and forth a couple of times to build up a swing. This swing is obtained while hanging on the knees by flexing slightly, bringing the arms up towards the thighs, and then reaching out with the arms and arching the upper body. After a couple of swings the dismount is done after passing the uprights and the body is at the peak of the front end of the swing. Lift the head and arms up and release the knees from the bar. Flex the hips and drop to the feet.

14. *Hock Swing with Half Twist.* As the performer swings up into the dismount he should turn his head and shoulders back into the direction of the twist. The knees are then released and the feet drop down toward the mat with the hips following the twisting action started by the head and shoulder. The dismount with the half twist is completed by landing on the mat in a standing position facing the bar. The hands may be placed on the bar for added balance.

15. *Front Hip Circle.* Start from a front support position. Straighten the arms and elevate the chest so that the thighs are resting on the bar. Fall forward and as the chest passes below the level of the bar, pull hard with the arms and continue the circle around the bar. Shift the wrists at the end so that the front support position is reached again. Try to keep the body in contact with the bar throughout the circle.

High Bar Stunts

The previously described stunts are those that are generally done on a horizontal bar that has been lowered to about chest height. Of course most of them can be done on an elevated high bar but for learning purposes they are considered low bar stunts. The next group of exercises are those that are done on a high horizontal bar. One of the first things that must be learned on a high bar is the technique of obtaining a proper swing. This will be described fully.

1. *Swing and Dismount.* Learning the proper technique of obtaining a swing and dismounting at the right moment on the back end of the swing is a very valuable skill to learn especially for beginners for whom it is the safest dismount. To obtain a swing from an ordinary hanging position, pull the body up toward the bar by a chinning action and at the same time lift the legs upward toward the bar. As the legs are lifted up above the level of the bar extend them outward and at the same time push with the arms and force an arch in the back. This action should provide a smooth even swing. The dismount is done at the back end of the swing. As the body swings by the uprights, pull slightly with

Start of front hip circle

Kip

the arms in an attempt to slow the swing a little and at the same time elevate the shoulders and try to keep the legs down as much as possible. This should have the effect of forcing the body in to a vertical position. When the very end of the backward swing is reached, the dismount is executed with a slight push of the hands and the subsequent drop to the feet.

2. *Kip.* Swing on the bar and towards the front end of the swing arch the body. After reaching the end of the front swing bring the feet up towards the bar. When the feet reach the bar and the hips are underneath it on the back swing, forcefully extend the legs upward and forward and pull hard with the arms. This kick and pull should kip the body up and forward into a straight arm support position above the bar. The spotter may assist by pushing under the hips as the

performer executes the kick action. An important item to remember is to wait until the body starts its backward movement before bringing the legs up for the kip. Many beginners start too early on the kip and end up by simply hitting the bar with the abdomen instead of passing around it.

Land Drill for Kip. A land drill that may be used in teaching the kip is to have the class lie on the floor or mats with their legs raised and the hands up near the ankles. The hands should pretend to be holding an imaginary bar. On a command all should sit up by extending the legs rocking the shoulders up to a sitting position and at the same time running the hands along the legs toward the hips. This emphasizes the need of keeping the legs near the bar throughout the kipping action of the stunt. If wands or broomsticks are available these

Tapping of foot on low bar kip

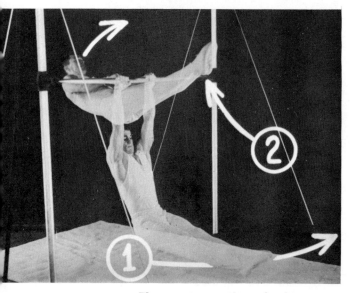

The one-two action of a kip

may be placed in the hands and drawn up towards the hips as the sit-up is completed.

Low Bar Kip. Another means of learning a kip is to work with the bar lowered to shoulder height. Start facing the bar with the hands in an overhand grip and at straight arm's distance. Jump up slightly with a pike of the body and then shoot the legs forward along the mats under the bar. At the end of the forward glide with the body completely extended drop one foot down to the mat and get a push with this foot while

lifting the other foot towards the bar (see first picture). After this tap with the lower foot then bring it up also, attempting to catch up to the other foot. When both feet reach the bar and the hips are under the bar kick the legs upward and outward and at the same time pull hard with the arms and execute the kipping action to a straight arm support position above the bar (see second picture).

3. *Circus Kip.* Another variation of a kip is commonly called a "circus kip." This consists of starting with a short swing and at the back end lift the hips slightly forcing a small pike in the hips. After this pike, swing forward extending the legs downward forcefully. This extension or beat should force an arch in the body as it swings forward. As the hips swing backward the legs are lifted up sharply toward the bar and at the same time the arms pull strongly. This extension and pull should snap the body upward into a straight arm support position above the bar. Again a spotter can be of great assistance by pushing under the hips as the circus kip is tried.

4. *Drop Kip.* From a straight arm support position above the bar swing backward and downward in a pike position. Keep the feet near the bar while swinging under the bar and allow the hips to swing downward, forward, and then backward. As the hips swing back kick the legs upward and pull with the arms and execute the drop kip into a straight arm support position.

5. *Back Uprise.* Obtain a high swing by lifting the legs up toward the bar and then casting them outward and at the same time push and extend the arms and body away from the bar. Swing through the bottom of the swing and just prior to the end of the backward swing pike slightly with the hips and pull hard

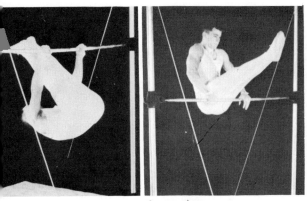

Seat rise

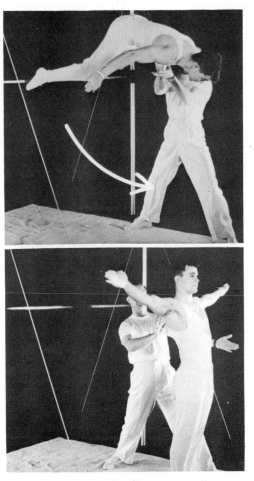

Sole circle dismount

with the arms. This pull and kipping action should lift the body up into the bar into a straight arm support position. A backward hip circle often follows the completion of this stunt.

6. *Seat Rise.* On the forward end of a swing bring both legs up in between the arms in either a tuck position or straight leg position. Allow the legs and feet to pass between the arms and under the bar and then shoot the feet up and forward over the top of the bar and at the same time pull hard with the arms. Finish in a sitting position on the bar supporting the body with the hands and the back of the thighs.

7. *Seat Rise Dismount.* This is similar to the seat rise mount, except after reaching the top of the mount continue the body over beyond the bar and land in a standing position on the mat on the other side of the bar. A stronger shoot of the legs over the top of the bar and a harder pull of the arms are necessary

in order to carry the entire body on into the dismount.

8. *Sole Circle Backward.* Start from a front straight arm support position. Flex the body slightly and then whip the legs up and place the feet on the bar outside of the hands in a straddle position. From

Sole circle backward

this position fall backward and make a complete circle holding on with the feet and hands. Keep a constant pressure on the bar with the feet and circle under the bar and up and over the top. Stretch out in back at the beginning and during the latter part of the circle pull in slightly and even bend the knees if necessary in order to complete the backward sole circle. You can execute this as a dismount by releasing your grip and lifting your shoulders and chest up just when you have almost completed the full sole circle. Then push forward off the bar with your feet and snap your legs under you.

9. *Sole Circle Forward.* Similar to the backward sole circle except the motion is forward. Start from the straight arm support position with the hands in a reverse grip. Whip the legs into a straddle position on the bar and from this position fall forward into a forward sole circle. Keep a constant pressure on the bar with the feet and pull strongly with the arms near the finish of the stunt.

10. *Reverse Kip.* The first part is similar to the swing and the shoot of the feet between the arms and under the bar as in the seat rise mount. Allow the feet to ride up part way in the back swing and then ride downward under the bar with the body remaining in a pike position. Just as the bottom of the swing is reached and the hips start to swing forward extend the body into an arched position with the head and shoulders pulling back and the legs extended downward. The hands shift as quickly as possible from a hanging position to a support position on top of the bar. Continue the reverse kip action until the body is in a back support position or a sitting position on top of the bar.

11. *Cast Cross Over to Back Uprise.* Start from a straight arm front support position with the hands in a regular grip position. Flex the hips slightly and then extend the body backward and upward and at the same time reach across the left hand with the right hand and grasp the bar on the left side of the hand. With the arms completely extended and the body stretched out swing the body under the bar. After the body has swung under the bar then turn naturally to the right in an untwisting action of the arms and at the same time pull with both arms. After the pull release the left hand first and regrasp the bar in a regular grip and then do the same with the right hand. Continue to pull with the hands and then complete the back uprise part of the stunt into a front support position on top of the bar. Often a back hip circle will follow this stunt as in the case of the ordinary back uprise.

12. *Half Giant Swing.* The regular half giant swing is started by grasping the bar with a regular grip and swinging back and forth a couple of times. On the last and biggest forward swing, swing the legs up and over the top of the bar. At the same time shift the hands from a hanging position to a support position on top of the bar. If this change of the hands is done soon enough the arms then catch the weight of the body and prevent unnecessary jolting of the abdomen while completing the last part of the half giant. An excellent practice for learning the shifting of the wrist from a hang to a support is to do free hip circles. This is simply a back hip circle with the body free of the bar while going through the backward circle. On this the stunt is started as an ordinary backward hip circle but the hands follow the stunt quickly and the weight remains constantly on them thus allowing the performer to hold the thighs away from the bar. This same action

once learned is used to do the half giant swing finish. After the under bar swing into a half giant has been tried a few times the half giant may be tried from a support position on top of the bar. Cast the legs up and away from the bar and then swing downward into the half giant circle. Shift the wrists early and catch the weight of the body as it completes its half giant action. Do this several times and as skill improves hold an arch throughout the half giant and execute a graceful back hip circle in finishing the stunt.

13. *Regular Giant Swing.* After the Regular Half Giant is learned the complete regular giant swing may be tried. This entails a high cast from the support position and a stronger swing throughout the stunt. A hard pull with the hands and a strong whip of the legs upward after the body circles through the bottom of the swing is essential. Pull with the hands and shift the wrists and continue circling the body upward into another hand stand position. This stunt may be tried in a belt or with the aid of spotters. It is important to cast high in the beginning, swing strong under the bar and whip the legs forcefully upward over the top of the bar. While learning bend the arms slightly so that the body can pass over the top of the bar easier. Remember that the finished stunt is done with the arms straight, body extended and arched, toes pointed, and so on.

14. *Reverse Half Giant Swing.* As in learning the regular giant swing there is a lead-up stunt for learning the Reverse Giant Swing. This stunt is simply called the Reverse Half Giant Swing. Start from a front support position on top of the bar with the hands in a reverse grip position. Flex the body slightly and then whip the legs over with the head and shoulders dropping slightly so that the

entire body swings over parallel to the mats and then into a half giant swing action. The feet and legs stretch out and the arms are extended into a smooth downward swing. The body continues downward and under the bar and back up the other side. The half giant finish is similar to the back uprise finish in that after the body has passed the uprights and has almost reached its peak at the back swing the hips are flexed a little and the arms pull strongly. This should bring the performer up to a straight arm support position above the bar as at the beginning.

15. *Reverse Giant Swing.* The Reverse Giant Swing is started from a front support position on top of the bar with the hands in reverse grip as in the reverse half giant swing. Flex the hips slightly and then whip the legs up and over the

Reverse giant swing

head and at the same time extend the arms so that the stunt is started in an almost straight hand balance position, from which the performer continues on over and downward into the full giant swing. Stretch out as much as possible and swing fully. On the back end of the swing, pull with the arms and kip the hips upward slightly. This will force the body upward into another hand balance position and from there on into another Reverse Giant Swing. Remember not to kip or pull with the arms too soon but instead wait for the moment when the body has almost reached the peak of the backward swing, then pull in toward the bar and allow the shoulders and head to shift over the bar and the feet to swing upward into the handstand position.

16. *Regular Flyaway.* A regular flyaway from the horizontal bar is one of the prettiest and yet one of the most difficult dismounts to master. Perhaps one of the easiest methods of learning this stunt is to use the "skin the cat" approach. By this it is meant that the first time a performer tries a flyaway he should simply hang on the bar and then pull the legs up and between the arms into a skin the cat position and then drop off to the feet. After a few times the stunt is then tried with a small swing but at all times the principle is the same in that a quick skin the cat is performed. The knees are bent and a slight pull of

the arms is effected. This principle is continued with the swing slightly increased with each try. Upon gaining confidence and sureness the flyaway is tried with more swing and later from a cast and finally from a giant swing. As swing increases, the body is extended to a layout position instead of a tuck. The spotters can assist by grasping the performer's wrists and helping him through the early stages of the dismount. An overhead safety belt can be of great help while learning the Regular Flyaway.

Routines

Some elementary routines for the high bar might include:

1. Belly grind, then a back hip circle into an underswing dismount forward.

2. Swing into a single leg swing-up, into a single leg circle backwards, continue below the bar disengaging the leg from the bar into a full swing with dismount at back end of swing.

3. Single leg swing-up, bring other leg over to sitting position into a back double knee circle, drop below bar into a back swing dismount.

4. Kip, into back hip circle, into under bar swing executing a half turn at front end of swing into single leg swing up into a front leg circle then bring front leg back and kip up into a sole circle dismount.

CHAPTER 9

Parallel Bars

PARALLEL BARS were first introduced by Friedrich Jahn in the early 1800's. He hoped through this apparatus and the several others that he invented to strengthen the degenerated muscle groups of the body and thus perhaps to liberate man from the shackles of an overcivilized environment that had enfeebled him.

The parallel bars consist of two parallel hand rails made of the finest grained hickory connected to uprights that are supported by a base consisting of two oval rails. All are firmly connected with no undue shaking allowed. The bars are adjustable in width and in height which allows convenient adjustment for the students of different age groups and sizes. For collegiate competition the bars should be from 5'3" to 5'7" high. The bars are 11'6" long with an inside width of 17" to 19". A competitive routine includes a series of stunts performed without touching the mat until the dismount.

VALUES

The specific values of working the parallel bars are:

1. The parallel bars develop strength and power in the arms, chest, and back.
2. Balance is essential to parallel bars work and is developed by it.
3. The maneuvers call for great coordination and timing.
4. Confidence is developed on the parallel bars.

ORGANIZATION

Area and Equipment

The parallel bars are easily moved and thus can be set up in any part of the gymnasium. Since the stunts do not require the performer to start or finish far away from the bars, the area needed would be that taken by the bars themselves plus about five feet on all sides. Mats should be under and around the bars. 5' × 10' mats will fit along the sides and ends but underneath and between the uprights is more of a problem where the same sized mats cannot be placed without curling up or overlapping, a practice which may cause injuries. The best solution is a special mat to fit the area. These can be obtained from the companies that supply parallel bars.

Teaching Methods

Normally only one person can work the parallel bars at one time, but during the elementary skills period, two performers may work at the same time. When doing dips, one student may work at each end. For a series of straddle seat travels the length of the bars, a second performer could begin before the first one had finished at the other end. Performers generally proceed quite rapidly so no undue waiting should result with large squads.

The instructor should carefully supervise the activity at the beginning stages since most students have a fear of falling between the bars. However, this fear is quickly overcome and with confidence the performer executes the stunts with little danger of injury.

The parallel bars can be evaluated very nicely by using a stunt chart. Because of the great variety of stunts possible, it might be easier and less time consuming to make up simple routines for checking purposes. For more advanced classes regular competitive routines make a good test.

Safety

In order to carry out a successful program of instruction on the parallel bars, a few safety hints should be followed:

1. Check the equipment to see that the floor rollers are released and that the pins are in the holes so that the bars will not slip down.

2. The area around and under the bars should be safely padded with mats.

3. In first working the parallel bars the bars should be lowered as far as possible. This makes for safe performance and convenient spotting. For balancing stunts a set of low parallel bars are extremely valuable to use.

4. One or more spotters should be present at all times to assist the performer through the more involved stunts.

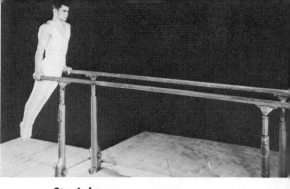

Straight arm support

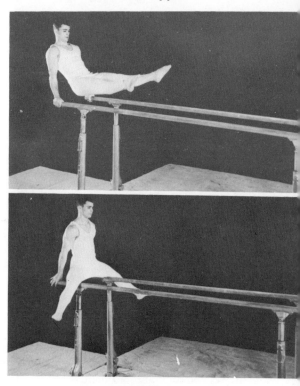

Jump to straddle seat

5. For stunts done in the middle of the bars, the spotter should stand to one side of the bars. In helping the performer, he should be careful not to allow the arm to be caught across the bars with the weight of the performer on the arm; thus most of the spotting should be done under the bars.

PROGRAM OF INSTRUCTION

There are three common starting positions:

(a) Straight arm support—jump onto

the bars with a hand on each bar. The arms are straight and run along the sides of the body. Keep the head up, chest out, body slightly arched, and the toes pointed.

(b) Straddle seat—from a straight arm support position, swing the legs forward between the bars. As the legs swing slightly above the bars, separate them and place one on each bar ending in a straddle seat position with the legs and back straight and the head and chest up and the hands behind the legs.

(c) Upper arm support—the body is supported between the bars by the upper arms which are over the bars. The hands grasp the bars ahead of the shoulders and the elbows are spread out to the side. The body should be able to swing freely from this position.

To become a successful performer on the parallel bars, it is important to progress slowly through the fundamental and strengthening stunts. As skill and strength improve, the more advanced stunts may be tried with complete confidence. The following is a description of some of the stunts that may be done on the parallel bars, given in a recommended order of progression. For variation, many of these stunts could be done in the opposite direction from the one described.

1. *Dips.* Jump onto the bars in a straight arm support position facing towards the center of the bars. In this position, flex the arms and drop downward until the elbow joint is less than a right angle. After reaching the bottom with the arms flexed, push the body upward into the straight arm position. Do several of these dips at one time to increase arm strength.

2. *Swing.* Jump to a straight arm support position on the ends of the bars, bring the legs up slightly and extend the

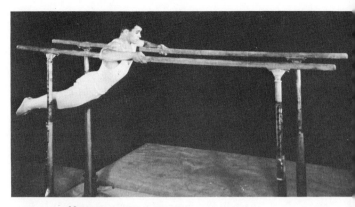

Upper arm support

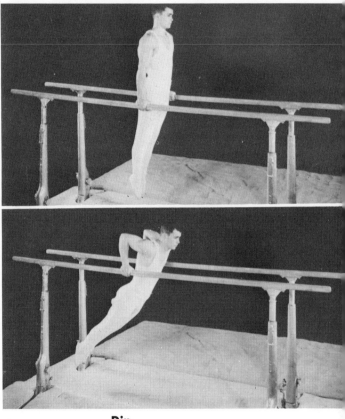

Dip

body into an arched position and then swing the legs downward and backward and forward in a series of swings. Be sure to keep the arms straight and make the *shoulders* the fulcrum of the swing.

Swing low at first and gradually increase the height of the swing. Control is especially important as the swing becomes larger.

3. *Swinging Dips.* Swing in a straight arm support position, and when the feet are at the end of the backward swing, flex the arms and drop to a dip position. Remain in this dip position as the legs swing forward. Just as the feet reach the end of the forward swing, push the arms straight and finish in a straight arm position. This same stunt can be done backwards by dropping into the full dip position at the end of the front swing and pushing up at the back end of the swing. To do this stunt on low parallel bars, it may be necessary to bend the knees so that the feet will not hit the mats.

4. *Swinging Dip Travel.* The first half of this stunt is done just like the swinging dips. As the body is swinging forward from the dip position, push vigorously with the arms in an upward and forward direction. The hands leave the bars momentarily, the body travels or hops forward, then the hands regrasp the bars, and the body finishes in a straight arm support position.

5. *Straight Arm Walk.* Walk the length of the bars in a straight arm support position, keeping the arms straight, head up, body arched. As one hand leaves the bar to take a step, shift the weight to the other hand. Be sure to take small steps with the hands.

6. *Front Support Turn.* From a straight arm support position in the center of the bars, lean to the right and shift the left hand to the right bar bringing the front of the thighs to rest against the bar. Keep the body straight and back slightly arched. Continue the turn by reaching back with the right hand and grasping the vacated bar thus ending in a straight arm support position.

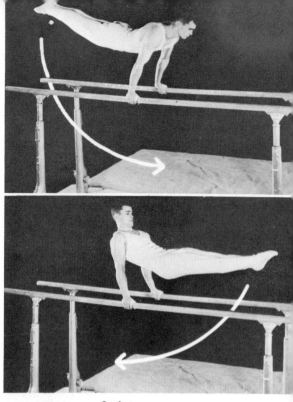

Swing

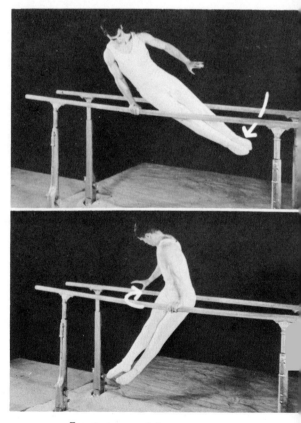

Front support turn

7. *Half Twist Change (Scissors from a Straight Arm Support).* Here is another simple method of turning around. From a straight arm support position swing both legs backward, execute a half twist of the body, and bring the right leg over the left bar and the left leg over the right bar. After finishing this scissor action, turn the body into a straddle seat position facing the opposite direction.

8. *Front Dismount.* Swing in the center of the bars from a straight arm support position. As the body reaches the peak of the backward swing and the legs are above the bars, push hard with the left arm and swing the body over the right bar so that the front part of the body is closest to the bar. After passing over this bar, drop toward the mat grasping the bar with the left hand as the right hand releases the grip. Land on the mat with the left hand steadying the landing by holding onto the closest bar.

9. *Rear Dismount.* Swing in the center of the bars in a straight arm support position. As the body swings forward and the feet reach a point above the bars, push with the left hand and swing the body over the right bar so that the rear of the body is closest to the bar. After

Front dismount

Rear dismount

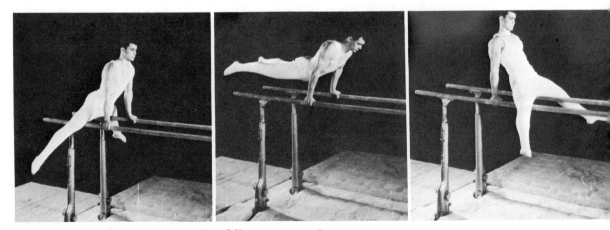

Straddle seat travel

Side seat half turn to straddle seat

passing over the right bar, regrasp it with the left hand as the right hand lets go.

10. *Straddle Seat Travel.* From a straddle seat position, lean forward and place the hands on the bars in front of the legs. As the weight is shifted to the

Single leg cut off—forward

straight arms, swing the legs backward above bar level; then bring them together and swing them forward between the bars. At the front of the swing, separate the legs again and place them in a straddle seat position in front of the hands. Travel the length of the bars in this manner.

11. *Side Seat Half Turn to Straddle Seat.* This stunt is a simple method of turning around and is done in the following manner. From a straight arm support position in the center of the bars, swing both legs forward over the right bar and end up in a side seat position. Release the right hand and place it on the left bar and bring the right leg across from the right bar over to the left bar. Bring the left hand back to the right bar and finish in a straddle seat position facing the opposite direction.

12. *Single Leg Cut Off—Forward.* This is a simple dismount. From a

Single leg cut on

Double leg cut on

Forward roll to straddle seat

straight arm support position on the end of the bars facing away from the bars, swing the body backward. At the back end of the swing, raise the hips and swing the right leg outside the right bar. On forward swing, release the right hand and land in a standing position on the mat. Remember to keep the shoulders well forward of the hands so that there is a definite forward lean into the dismount which will help to keep the cutting leg from hitting the bar.

13. *Single Leg Cut On.* Stand on the mats facing the end of the bars and grasp them with the hands. Jump

toward a straight arm support position and as the body moves forward, separate the legs and pass the left leg outside of the left hand. The left leg passes over the bar to the inside of the bars while the performer releases the left hand. After the leg has passed over the bar, regrasp the bar and finish in a straight arm position. When first attempting this stunt, cut the leg across the bar without regrasping and land in a standing position on the mat until the proper cutting action is achieved. Two more stunts of this type are the Single Leg Cut Off Backward and the Double Leg Cut Off Backward. Both of these start from a straight arm support position facing the center of the bars.

14. *Forward Roll to Straddle Seat.* Start from a straddle seat position and grasp the bars in front of the thighs. Lean forward and place the upper arms on the bars with the elbows out to the side. Raise hips, keeping the body in a pike position. As the hips pass over the head, release the hands keeping the elbows out to the side and grasp the hands behind the back. The roll is continued to a straddle seat position.

Backward straddle shoulder roll

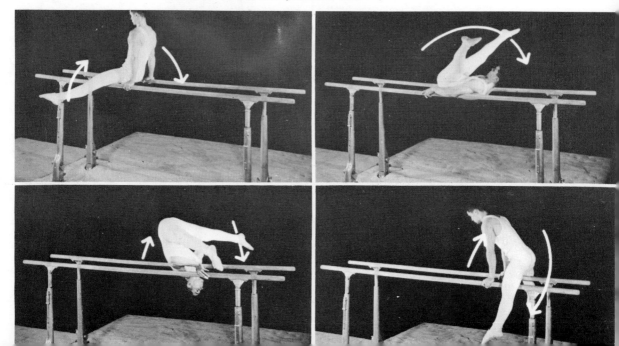

15. *Backward Straddle Shoulder Roll.* From a straddle seat position lean backwards onto the arms and execute a backward roll. Grasp the bars over the shoulders and continue the roll to a straddle seat.

16. *Back Roll Off Both Bars Dismount.* Start from a sitting position on one bar with the hands grasping it on each side of the hips and the body facing away from the bars. Lean backward so the back rests on the other bar and bring the legs up and over the head. When the feet are as far down towards the mats as possible, release the hands and land on the mats in a standing position.

17. *Lazy Man's Kip.* Grasp the ends of the bars and jump up, placing the feet about half way up on each of the uprights. Swing the body downward, flexing the knees, and hang on with the hands. When the swing reaches the point where the knees are fully flexed, start the return swing upward by straightening the legs and pulling forcefully with the arms. Continue this pull and shift the wrists from a hanging position to a support position and finish in a straight arm support position.

18. *Shoulder Balance (Upper Arm Balance).* Start from a straddle seat position and grasp the bars in front of the thighs. Lean forward and place the upper arms on the bars with the elbows out to the side. Raise the hips and extend the legs over the head. Assume the shoulder balance position with the back arched, head up, and toes pointed with the elbows out to the side. Either slowly return the body to the starting position or pike the body and roll to a straddle seat. A spotter is important in first learning this stunt.

19. *Single Leg Circle Forward.* From a straight arm support position in the

Shoulder balance

middle of the bars, swing the right leg forward over the left bar. Follow with the right hand. Transfer the left hand to the opposite bar and continue the right leg so that it ends between the bars. Finish in a straight arm support position facing the opposite direction. Remember to transfer the body weight to the left bar during the change.

20. *Shoulder Balance—Side Dismount.* From a shoulder balance, lean to the right and push off with the left hand, allowing the body to rotate around the right bar and land in a standing position on the mat. Hold on with the right hand in order to steady the landing. This dismount has the same feeling as doing a cartwheel.

21. *Belly Grind Mount.* Stand facing the bars with arms under the near bar and the hands grasping the far bar in a regular grasp. Take a step under the bars and kick upward with the feet, pulling the abdomen into the bar with the legs going on over the top of the bars. Push body up to a front leaning rest position across the bars. Swing the right leg between the bars and then over the right bar ending up in a straddle seat position.

Front uprise

22. *Back Uprise.* This stunt must be done with the bars at least as high as the performer's shoulders when standing. From an upper arm support position, swing back and forth a couple of times. On the back end of one of the swings, pull hard with the hands and lift the hips upward. Continue the pull which brings the shoulders forward and finish in a straight arm support position. A fairly high swing helps in the accomplishment of this stunt.

23. *Front Uprise.* From an upper arm support position, swing back and forth a couple of times. Towards the end of

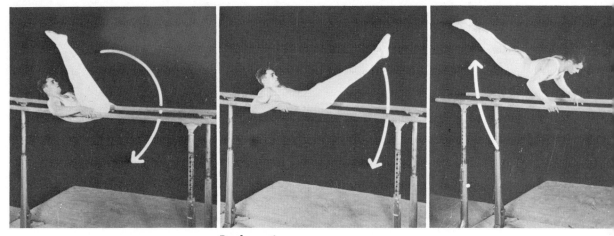

Back uprise

Straddle forward dismount

the forward swing, pull hard with the hands and thrust the hips forward and lift the feet. Continue the pull and finish in a straight arm support position. If the performer has difficulty, he could finish in a straddle seat position a couple of times before attempting the regular ending. A spotter can help by pushing under the hips.

24. *Scissors Change from Straddle Seat.* Start in a straddle seat position with both hands behind the legs. Swing the right leg between the bars and transfer the left hand to the right bar. As right leg swings vigorously backward, put the weight on the hands. Remove the left leg from the left bar and swing it over to the opposite bar, with the right leg moving over to the left bar. Finish in a straddle seat position facing the opposite direction with the hands behind the body.

25. *Straddle Forward Dismount.* From a straight arm support position on the end of the bars facing away from the bars, swing the legs backward. On the back end of the swing, raise the hips and swing the feet outside of the bars into a straddle position. Cut the legs for-

ward sharply, releasing both hands and allow the legs to pass over the ends of the bars. Finish in a standing position on the mat. Remember to maintain a definite forward lean throughout the stunt. The spotter may grab the performer's shoulder or the upper arm and help him clear the bars by pulling forward.

26. *Rear Vault Dismount with Half Twist.* From a straight arm support position between the bars, start the body swinging. On the forward end of the swing, lift the legs up and over one bar as in the rear vault. As the body clears the bar, execute a half twist towards the bar. End in a standing position facing the opposite direction with the near hand on the bar.

27. *Top Kip to Straddle Seat.* From an upper arm support position in the middle of the bars, raise the legs forward

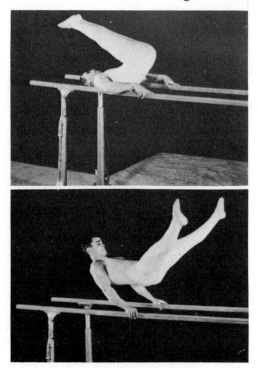

Top kip to straddle seat

Swing to shoulder balance

Straddle leg cut on to straddle seat

between the bars and over the head so that the body is in a pike position. From this pike position, extend the legs forward, and separating them and at the same time pull hard with the arms. Finish in a straddle seat position above the bars. Be sure to get the hips high over the bars prior to doing the kip as this will help in the execution of the stunt. A spotter can help by pushing under the hips as the kip is executed.

28. *Top Kip.* This stunt is done the same way as the top kip to a straddle seat except that the legs are kept together throughout the stunt and thus the finish is into a straight arm support position.

29. *Swing to Shoulder Balance.* Start in a straight arm support position and swing back and forth a couple of times. At the end of the back swing, flex the arms and drop the shoulders forward toward the bars, keeping the body straight. Place the upper arm on the bars, remembering to keep the body arched and head up. Finish in a shoulder balance position.

30. *Top Kip to Shoulder Balance.* As the top kip is completed, keep the body rotating forward. As the momentum causes a forward lean, flex the arms, drop the shoulders to the bars and allow the feet to rise over the head to a shoulder balance position.

31. *Straddle Leg Cut On to Straddle Seat.* As in the Single Leg Cut On, grasp the ends of the bars and jump upward, straddling both legs over the bars and land in a straddle seat position on the bars.

32. *Straddle Leg Cut On to Straight Arm Support.* Same as the above except the legs continue over the bar and finish together and hands grasp the bars in a straight arm support position. The spotter can grab the back of the per-

former's trunks and give him a boost.

33. *End Kip.* With the hands on the ends of the bars, swing the legs forward and up to a pike position, hanging underneath the bar. As the body swings backward after the forward swing, extend the legs upward, pull with the arms, and finish in a straight arm support position above the bars.

34. *Glide Kip.* This stunt may be done from the end of the bars or in the middle of the bars. It is very similar to the end kip except for the glide part. At the beginning, have the feet skim over the mats until the front end of the swing is reached. Then bring the legs up to a pike position, and kip upward with the legs and pull strongly with the arms and finish in a straight arm support position between the bars.

35. *Double Rear Dismount.* From a straight arm support position, swing the body. At the end of the back swing, lift the hips and swing both legs over the left bar. Continue the legs over the right bar and down towards the mats where the dismount finishes in a standing position. Remember to keep the weight of the body on the right arm as the dismount is executed to the right. Keep the hips fairly high throughout the dismount. A spotter may assist by grasping the right arm of the performer pulling slightly while the stunt is being tried.

36. *Backward Giant Roll (Shoulder Roll).* This stunt consists basically of completing a full backward roll of the body in a layout position with the arms supporting the weight on the bars. From an upper arm support position with the hands grasping the bars in front of the chest, swing the legs back and forth a couple of times. Obtain a forceful swing downward and allow the feet to continue on up and over the head. When

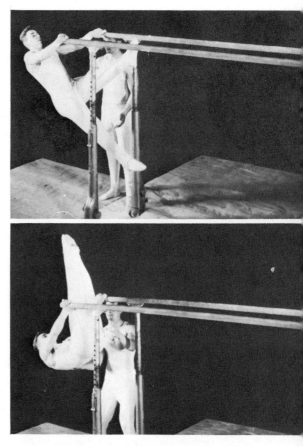

End kip

Backward giant roll

the hips reach the height of the bars, push hard with the hands and release the grip and throw the arms straight out at the sides. With the head back and body arched, allow the legs and feet to continue on over past the vertical position and on down toward the original position between the bars. When the feet are directly overhead and are just starting to continue downward, the hands reach forward and grasp the bars. By grasping the bars, the performer is able to steady the downward flow of the roll. As proficiency increases in this stunt, the backward giant roll may be tried from a shoulder balance position. Two or three of these in a row make for a fine performance.

37. *Cast.* This stunt can be done from a straight arm support position above the bars or from a standing position on the mats between the bars. From a standing position on the mats, grasp the bars with each hand on the inside of the bar and the fingers circling the top side of the bar. Lean backward and jump up slightly off the mat, keeping the arms straight and bringing the legs up so the body is in a pike position. Allow the body to swing downward between the bars, reaching the full bottom of the swing and start the upward swing. Just before reaching the peak of the forward swing, extend the body forcefully forward by shooting the legs up between the bars and pulling strongly with the arms. Continue this extension of the body with the legs pressing forward until the shoulders move above the height of the bars. At this point extend the arms to the side and finish in an upper arm support position. Allow the feet then to swing downward and at the back end of the swing execute a back uprise to a straight arm support position. To do the cast from a straight arm sup-

Cast

port position, raise the legs slightly and drop backward between the bars. This puts the performer in a pike position swinging beneath the bar which is correct for completing the cast.

38. *Dip Half Turn.* Execute a swinging dip movement and on the upward swing with the body in a slightly piked position, extend an arch in the body, push hard with the hands, and execute a half twist either to the left or right. Upon completion of the half turn regrasp the bars in a straight arm support position. Try this stunt on the low bars at first.

39. *Swing to a Hand Balance.* After learning a hand balance on the low parallel bars by kicking up from the mat, the performer should try a hand balance from a swing on the higher bars. At first, do this on the end of the bars facing outward so that the performer can land safely if he swings beyond the balance position. This can be done by lifting one hand and twisting the body around to face the bars like doing a round off on the mats. As for doing the hand balance, swing from the shoulders with the arms straight from a straight arm support position. When ready to swing to the hand balance, arch at the front end of the swing and keep the body arched throughout the back swing. Allow the feet to swing over the head, keeping the shoulders over the hands. Flex the arms slightly if needed. If going off balance, grip hard with the hands to maintain the balance and don't give up easily. (*Safety precaution*—in coming down from the hand balance, do not allow the body to swing freely back to the straight arm support position. Slow down the swing with the shoulders and upper back muscles.)

40. *Moore.* Swing in a straight arm support position. As the body passes the hands on the back swing, lift the hips into the air and jackknife the body.

Reach backward with the left hand toward the right bar and continue to keep the hips high turning to the left so that the body is facing in towards both bars. Allow the feet to swing on the outside of the right bar and with the left hand on the right bar fairly near the right hand, circle the legs on around the right bar keeping the hips high throughout. After the feet reach the midpoint in the circle around the outside of the right bar, release the right hand and reach across and grasp the

Hand balance

Moore

free bar. Then let the feet pass over the right bar and swing them down between the two bars. This can be spotted effectively with an overhead safety belt rigging. Simply cross the ropes in the proper direction behind the performer's back and follow the Moore through by pulling the rope supporting the performer.

41. *Front Overbar Somersault.* From a straight arm support position, swing several times. When a maximum swing is obtained on the backward swing, lift the hips upward and forward in a pike position. Push off hard with the hands and duck the head. Keep the arms spread and land on the upper arms and regrasp. Later on, this may be done to a catch in the straight arm support position. It should be tried first from a small swing into a simple forward roll.

42. *Front Overbar Somersault Dismount.* The basic principle of the somersault is similar to the Front Overbar within the bars except it is done over one bar in a dismount fashion to the mats. Be sure to look over the dismounting bar just prior to somersaulting. Push with the far hand in order to move the body over the bars towards the mat. Regrasp the bar with the inside hand as quickly as possible in order to steady the landing. While first learning it is suggested that the bar over which the dismount is tried be padded. An overhead belt may be used or careful hand spotting applied.

43. *Pirouette.* From a handstand, change the left hand forward to the right bar and quickly change the right hand back to the left bar. End up in a handstand facing the opposite direction. Keep the body stretched out during the change of hands so that the shift in weight will take place without loss of balance. This stunt should be mastered on the low parallel bars before attempting it on the higher bars.

Front overbar somersault dismount

44. *Back Uprise to a Cut and Catch and Swing to a Handstand.* From a top kip position on the parallel bars, the body is extended upward and forward as far as possible. The purpose of this phase of the stunt is to get a maximum swing. After the body passes the bottom of the swing and starts upward, the arms start to pull. When the legs are above the bars, they spread quickly and the hands give a strong quick pull and then release which enables the legs to pass under the hands and continue the straddle vault to meet in front of the body in a momentary half lever position. After the legs pass under the arms, the hands reach downward toward the bars. When they catch the bars in the straight arm support position the body then swings up into the handstand. Some points to remember on this stunt are: (1) Obtain a maximum swing for this stunt. (2) When the legs straddle over the bars, do this as quickly as possible. (3) Try to have the hips forward of the arms when catching the bars after the vault. This enables an easy swing to a handstand. (4) This is usually done to a straight arm catch but can be done to a bent arm catch as well.

45. *Underbar Somersault (Peach Basket) to Upper Arm Support Position.* Start this stunt from a standing position between the bars with the hands grasping the inside of the bars. Jump upward and after reaching the top of your height, fall backward with the arms straight and start to pike the body. When the body passes the bottom of the downward swing and starts up, extend the body into an arch and at the same time pull with the hands. Upon releasing with the hands swing the arms up in between and over the parallel bars, landing on the upper arms and allowing the body to swing forward naturally.

This stunt is actually a preliminary one for the more advanced stunt of an underbar somersault to a straight arm support position. Some pointers are: (1) Keep the hips high throughout the trick. Do not let them drop too far backwards and below the bars. (2) When underneath the bar and executing the last part of the stunt, be sure not to release the hands too soon. An early release of the hands causes the body to travel and prevents a neat looking finish to the stunt.

46. *Back Overbar Somersault to Catch.* As pictured, this stunt is executed from a handstand. The body is then allowed to swing downward between the bars with a natural arch. This swing should be free and easy and definitely not tight or tense. The arms should be kept straight and the shoulders should be slightly forward of the hands.

After passing between the arms, the body in a slightly piked position should extend to an arched position with the head and shoulders extended backward. This is the key spot in the entire stunt. Here we must watch for a few faults which are as follows: (1) Don't lean forward or backward excessively. (2) Don't bend the arms. (3) Don't release the bars with your hands too soon. (Rather, allow them to be pulled off by the momentum of the swing.)

After the hands are pulled from the bars by the upward and backward momentum of the body, they should reach backward for the catch position. As soon as the bars are caught, allow the body to continue its natural swing and finish in the straight arm support position.

In learning this stunt, it is recommended that an overhead safety belt be used. This eliminates many unnecessary bruises and jolts in learning the fundamentals of the stunt. The overhead belt also overcomes fear of the stunt and in return develops confidence which is so essential to the successful gymnast. It is also suggested that this stunt be done first on lowered parallel bars with the suggested height being several inches below the performer's arm pits when he is standing on the mats.

Back overbar somersault to catch

CHAPTER 10

Rings

THE FLYING AND STILL RINGS have always had an air of adventure and daring, since Francis Amores of Spain invented this event along with the flying trapeze in the early 1800's. From the rings one can easily imagine himself an acrobat performing high above a crowd in a great circus tent. Along with this feeling of adventure there is great enjoyment and fun in swinging back and forth on a set of flying rings.

The rings, approximately eight inches in diameter, are wooden or may be steel with a rubber or leather covering. Adjustable straps about three feet in length are attached to the rings from steel cables which in turn are attached to a beam 18 feet above the floor for still rings and 24 feet above the floor for flying rings. A safety chain besides the metal alcove attachment should be added from the beam to the end of the cable. The rings themselves are about 8' above the floor. Both still and flying rings competition calls for a routine of successive stunts performed without returning to the mat until the dismount. Flying ring work is done with a swinging of the rings whereas still ring work is intended to be done with the rings motionless.

VALUES

The specific values of working on the rings are:

1. Rings develop strength in the muscles of the arms and chest. This is especially true of still rings work with its presses, levers, and difficult balances.

2. Because the rings must be gripped in the hands, strength in the fingers and a good grip are developed.

3. Ring work develops a sense of rhythm and beat, especially on the flying rings.

4. Working on the rings develops suppleness within the shoulder joints due to stunts involving twisting and turning of the arms while the joint is extended.

5. Swinging at great heights and performing stunts involving intricate timing develops confidence in the ability to handle one's body under such circumstances.

6. Due to the nature of the activity, still rings particularly can be worked by certain handicapped people giving them enjoyment and a feeling of accomplishment. Most stunts on the rings involve the upper body with the legs only being swung to give momentum. Men whose legs have limited use have been known to win championships.

ORGANIZATION

Area and Equipment

Since the rings are in a fixed position, they cannot be moved at will around the gymnasium. Still rings require very little floor area with a 5′ × 10′ mat being satisfactory padding underneath. Flying rings need much more space. Figuring the arc of a swinging 16 foot rope plus extra linear space for dismounting, a minimum of 30 feet of floor space should be kept clear underneath the rings. Of course, this area should be padded.

Teaching Methods

Because only one person can work at a time on the rings and because most schools will not have more than two or three sets of rings, the squad method is best used for instruction. Stunts on the still rings are difficult, and the trials will proceed rapidly since generally one stunt at a time is tried. Much more time will be spent per individual on the flying rings because of the swing.

While first participating in this activity the rings should be lowered to approximately shoulder height. As skill progresses the rings may be elevated to the regulation competitive height of about eight feet from the floor.

The instructor or squad leader should constantly stand to one side of the performer while the stunts are being attempted. The instructor can then assist the performer through the stunts and can also catch him in case of a slip or fall.

It is advisable to learn the stunts first on the still rings before trying them on the flying rings. Although the momentum produced by the swing makes the stunt less strenuous to perform, the tim-ing is more important and the danger of injury greater. Also, it is much easier to assist and spot on the still rings.

Evaluation of performers on the rings can be done by means of a stunt chart with competitive routines serving this purpose in advanced classes.

Safety

Because of the height involved, spotting is more difficult on the rings than on other pieces of apparatus. Also, the fact that the full body weight is supported by the hand grip leaves some danger of falling. Many stunts involve a strain on the shoulders, which leaves some danger of shoulder injuries if improperly performed. However, if instruction is carried out using a progressive order of learning and the activity is closely supervised, it is not a dangerous activity.

Some hints for the safe conduct of this activity are:

1. Use mats along the entire length of the swing.
2. Use carbonate of magnesia chalk on the hands before working.
3. When dropping off the flying rings, always do so from the back end of the swing and not the front.
4. Use a traveling overhead safety belt when learning difficult dismounts on the flying rings.
5. Don't swing too high or too long.
6. Periodically check the rings, straps, cables, and connections for weak spots.

PROGRAM OF INSTRUCTION

Still Rings

As suggested the rings should first be worked at approximately shoulder height and as a still ring event. Some of the stunts that can be done on the still rings

Chin-up L position

Chin-up one arm to the side

Pike hang

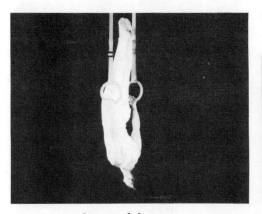

Inverted hang

and in the recommended order of progression are as follows.

1. *Chin-Ups.* Grasp the rings and simply pull up into a chin-up position. Repeat.

2. *Chin-Ups with Legs in L Position.* Raise the legs to an L position parallel to the mats and execute a chin-up.

3. *Chin-Up—One Arm to the Side.* Execute a chin-up and while the arms are in the flexed position, extend one to the side then bring it back and then extend the other arm to the side.

4. *Pike Hang.* Grasp the rings and bending at the hips bring the feet up and over the head. Finish in a jackknife position with the knees straight and close to the chest. This is a fundamental starting position for many ring stunts.

5. *Inverted Hang.* Grasp the rings and bring the feet up and over the head. Finish with the legs straight above the performer between the rings with the feet together, body arched, and arms straight. Hold this position for balance for a few seconds and then return to the original starting position. At first it may be tried with the legs resting on the straps.

6. *Bird's Nest.* Grasp the rings with the hands and pull the feet up and into the rings. Place the instep in the rings and arch the body so the chest is facing

Bird's nest

the mat. Hold for a moment and return.

7. *Bird's Nest—One Foot.* Do the bird's nest and remove one foot from the ring, extending that leg straight out behind.

8. *Bird's Nest—One Foot and One Hand.* Do the bird's nest and remove one foot and then release opposite hand and hold the position with only one hand and one foot.

9. *Skin the Cat.* Grasp the rings and bring the legs up between the arms and continue them on over to an extended position with the toes reaching downward as far as possible towards the mat. Return to original position.

10. *Monkey Hang.* Do the skin the cat and while in an extended position, release one arm and complete a full turn on the arm and return to a hanging position on both rings. Be sure to be completely extended in the skin the cat position before releasing.

11. *Single Leg Cut Off—Forward.* Grasp the rings and bring both legs up into a pike position between the rings. Swing forward with both legs and at the same time spread them apart so as

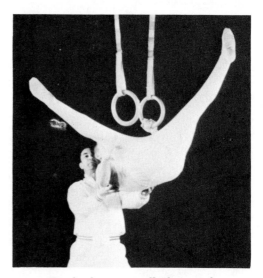

Single leg cut off—forward

to cut one leg between a ring and a hand. Release the ring with the hand and allow the leg to pass between and then regrasp the ring. While doing the single leg cut off, the arms should be in a slightly flexed position as this will give added control to the stunt. The head and shoulders should be rolled up towards the rings before cutting off for a safer and easier execution of the stunt.

Dislocate

Spotting a dislocate

12. *Double Leg Cut Off—Forward.* Same as single leg cut off except that both legs are swung between one ring and hand. Regrasp the ring after the legs pass between it and the hand. The spotter should stand behind the performer for this stunt.

13. *Jump to Straight Arm Support.* Grasp the rings and jump upward into a straight arm support position above the rings. Keep the arms near the side of the body while in the straight arm support position above the rings. The rings in this particular stunt should be at shoulder height.

14. *Dislocate.* Grasp the rings and bring the legs up so that the body is in a pike position. From this position extend the legs up and backwards and at the same time push the arms out to the side and arch the body. With the arms completely out to the sides and the body in an arched position dislocate the shoulders and swing the feet on towards the mat. Allow the feet to continue toward the mat to a standing position or bend the legs and swing on through to the original pike position. Just as the dislocate is completed pull up slightly with the arms as this will absorb the shock or strain at the completion of the stunt. This is done only at first while learning the stunt as when it is mastered the arms should be straight throughout. Assistance in this stunt is accomplished by the instructor lifting up on the shoulders and by holding the legs parallel to the mat until the dislocation of the shoulders is completed.

15. *Inlocate.* From a pike position swing the legs forward, downward and

Inlocate

backward. At the peak of the backward swing turn the arms inward, drop the head forward and pike the body and inlocate to a pike position. Assistance can be given by lifting up on the legs as the performer swings into the pike.

16. *Kip to Straight Arm Support*. From a pike position under the rings, extend the legs upward and forward and pull with the arms. Continue the kip until the body is above the rings in a straight arm support position with the shoulders and arms resting against the straps. The spotter may assist by pushing upward under the hips of the student.

17. *Forward Roll*. From a straight arm support position above the rings roll forward slowly into a pike position below the rings. Be sure to elevate the hips as the head is dropped forward prior to the roll. Lower the body slowly by keeping the arms flexed as the roll is completed.

18. *Back Uprise*. The rings should be elevated to the regulation height of about eight feet while trying this stunt. Bring the legs up into a pike position and then extend them forward and downward. Continue the swing of the legs under the rings and as the legs swing backward pull with the arms and finish above the rings in a straight arm

Back uprise

Kip to straight arm support

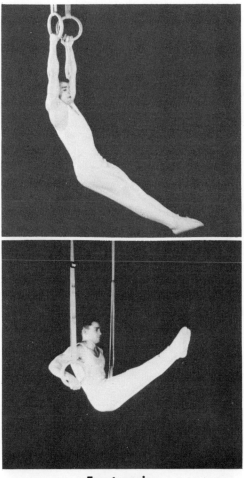

Front uprise

support position. A forceful downward swing is of great importance in executing this stunt.

19. *Front Uprise.* This stunt can be first tried on the still rings at the regular elevated height of 8'. Swing the feet back and forth a couple of times and at the back end of one of the swings pike slightly and then beat the feet downward directly below the point of suspension. After the beat allow the feet to swing backwards and then forward. At the front end of the swing pike slightly and start pulling with the arms. After a quick pike of the body extend the legs downward and thrust the upper body up towards the rings. Pull hard with the arms and on the way up to a position above the rings shift the wrists from a hanging position to that of a support position. Straighten the arms and finish in a straight arm support position.

20. *Shoulder Balance.* From a straight arm support position bend forward lifting the hips above the head and flex the arms so that the shoulder balance position can be reached. Keep the head up and slowly lift the feet upward to a straight shoulder balance position. Hold

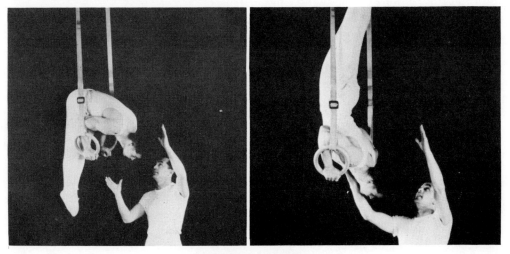

Shoulder balance

an arch in the body and point the toes. The arms should be flexed enough so that the upper arms may apply pressure against the straps in order to maintain the balance. Spotter should be used in learning this stunt. Also, the feet may be placed along the ropes during the learning period.

21. *Reverse Kip.* Grasp the rings and swing the feet back and forth a couple of times. Finally as the feet swing forward continue them on upwards between straps of the rings. Shoot the feet into the air and attempt to change the grip of the hands from a hanging position to a support position above the rings. In learning this stunt it might be advisable to think of it as a high dislocate and try to stop the dislocate half way through and catch the body above the rings in a support position. The spotter can assist by pushing upward under the performer's shoulders as he attempts the shoot into the reverse kip. Be sure to finish with the rings in front of the body and not behind the hips.

Flying Rings

Most of the stunts described for the still rings can be done on the flying rings and so it is suggested that almost all stunts be learned first on the still rings and later tried on flying rings. This will provide for safety in performance and easier spotting.

1. *Swinging on Flying Rings.* Learning to swing properly on flying rings is a very important basic skill and should be practiced diligently. Hang freely with the hands on the rings, swing back and forth a few times, and try to obtain a proper beat. This should be done by piking slightly at the back end of the swing and beat downward with the feet at the center of the swing directly below the point of suspension.

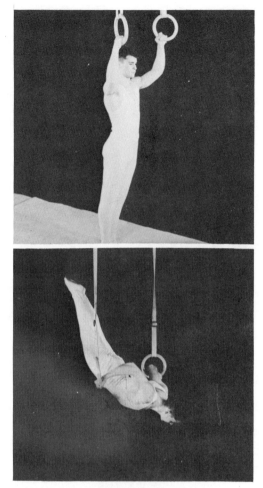

Reverse kip

The feet then swing back and then forward and upward at the front end of the swing. After the peak of the front swing is reached swing the feet backward as the swing starts backward. After the feet have swung backward allow them to swing forward so they reach the bottom of the swing just as the rings pass again over the center of the swing directly above the suspension point. This beat is continued, remembering always to extend or beat the feet downward at the center of the ring swing which is directly above the suspension point. As mentioned, in order to acquire

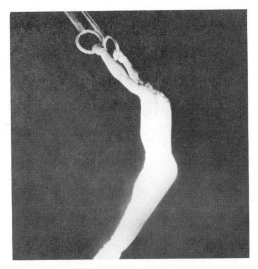

Piking for the beat

the correct swing and beat, considerable practice is essential but once it has been learned many stunts can then be accomplished.

Techniques of Giving a Swing. There are many ways of giving a performer a swing on the flying rings. Often a certain section of the country is identified with a particular method while another method is closely akin with another section of the country. Some consistently use a method of simply running under the performer and pushing with the hands; another area might use a method of standing on a tower of adequate height, like a flying trapeze perch, placed at the end of the swinging area and by grasping the rings and then jumping off the tower into the swing, the performer obtains the proper momentum. Another method which has proven to be quite successful is simply a system of grasping the ankles and swinging the performer into the swing. In detail the system consists of grasping one of the performer's ankles and with the free hand pushing him forward on the hips. When the ring man reaches the end of his forward swing then the swinger grasps both ankles, runs backward pulling the performer with him. When he reaches a point on the backward swing where the performer's ankles are slightly above his shoulders then he thrusts the performer forward into the swing. In thrusting the performer's feet forward, attempt to place the feet as far forward as possible, simulating the first part of an ordinary swing with the feet beating downward at a spot below the point of suspension. The performer can help the swinger a great deal by piking the body slightly in the back end of the swing while the swinger is preparing to thrust him forward. Another hint is to maintain a taut body especially the legs while the swinger throws the legs forward into the swing. With practice this method of giving a swing can be successful and effective.

2. *Front Uprise.* This stunt is done at the front end of the swing. While swinging forward from the back end of a swing, beat downward with the feet at the center of the swing. After this beat allow the feet to ride backward and then forward and just prior to reaching the end of the front swing pull with the arms and thrust the hips forward and upward and extend the feet up and then downward. Continue the pull until the body is above the rings in a straight arm support position.

3. *Cast.* From a straight arm support position above the rings extend the legs backward and push with the arms just prior to reaching the end of the backward swing. Continue the cast until the body is below the rings in a free swinging position.

4. *Back Uprise.* Swing backward with the body in a pike position and just before the end of the back swing is reached, extend the legs downward forcefully, and pull hard with the arms

and finish in a straight arm support position above the rings.

5. *One and a Half Reverse Roll.* This stunt is done at the front end of the swing. The performer beats down while swinging forward at the spot directly under the point of suspension. Allow the feet to continue backward and then forward as the end of the swing is reached. As the feet come forward the performer brings his legs up into a pike position at the same time a slight pull of the arms is affected. Rotating the body backward the performer completes a full turn and continues another half so the body ends in a hanging pike position. At this point the backward swing is commenced and the performer remains in this piked position through the remainder of the backward swing in preparation for another stunt at the end of the back swing.

6. *Dislocate on Swinging Rings.* Essentially the dislocate itself is done the same as described previously on the still rings. Some added hints: prepare for the dislocate by starting to extend into the dislocate just prior to reaching the back end of the swing. This will produce a free and easy dislocate which will have an air of flow and continuity about it. Work with the swing and the dislocate will be one of the most beautiful stunts performed on the rings.

7. *Inlocate on Swinging Rings.* This, too, is done essentially as described on the still rings. The movement becomes more graceful and rhythmical when performed with the benefit of a swing.

8. *Kip Forward Roll.* The performer swings forward in a pike position. Just prior to reaching the end of the forward swing the legs are dropped deeper into the pike position which then provides a spring-like action for the kip roll at the end of the swing. The performer simply executes a kip and reaching the height of the rings with his shoulders the head is dropped downward into the roll. The body remains in a pike position throughout the kip roll. The arms extend sidewards and turn inwards towards the roll. With practice this stunt can be executed in an extremely elegant and graceful manner.

9. *Reverse Kip on Back End of Swing.* Swing forward and raise the legs into a partial pike position. Hold this position momentarily until after the backward swing has started. Swing the legs downward and then forward as the performer swings back through the backward swing. At the end of the backward swing allow the feet to swing forward and thus up and over the head and into the reverse kip. Remember a correct beat is essential in accomplishing this stunt. Practice the beat several times before attempting the entire reverse kip. For more details on the reverse kip see the stunt as done on the still rings.

10. *Shoot to Shoulder Balance.* Swing forward and beat with the feet at the center of the swing. Allow the feet to

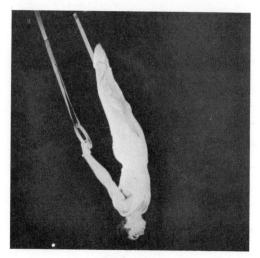

Dislocate

Dismounting at rear end of swing

Straddle dismount forward

swing backward and then forward. As the feet swing forward and the end of the forward swing is almost reached bring the legs up over the head and extend them up above the rings and between the straps. As the legs ride into the air and the body is lifted above the rings, pull with the arms and change the hand grip from a hanging grasp to a support position above the rings. Keep the shoulders low and settle quickly into a comfortable shoulder balance. Keep the head up, arch the back and work the arms in order to maintain the balance.

Dismounts

There are several methods of dismounting from the rings and those listed below are the ones used most often. Remember to exercise a reasonable amount of caution and care in learning these dismounts since if they are poorly executed or carelessly attempted injuries can and will occur.

1. *Dismount at Rear End of Swing.* This is a simple act of releasing the rings at the end of the backward swing and dropping to the feet. Remember in this stunt, keep the body in a straight vertical position before releasing the hands. Also pull with the arms slightly just prior to dropping. Try to dismount at the very end of the backward swing as this will enable the body to drop straight downward to a standing position on the mats.

2. *Dismount at Front End of Swing.* Swing past the center and as the front end of the swing is approached execute a half twist of the body. As the half twist is completed, pull up slightly with the arms and then release the rings and drop to the feet.

3. *Straddle Dismount Forward.* This stunt is started from a pike position. At the peak of the back swing pull with the hands and whip both legs forward and at the same time spread them apart so as to straddle the rings. Release the rings and allow the legs to pass outside of the rings. Continue the motion of the legs forward and downward until they reach a vertical position and then continue to drop to a standing position on the mat. To facilitate the learning of the stunt the head and shoulders should be rolled up towards the rings before releasing the hands.

Straddle dismount backward

Regular flyaway

4. *Straddle Dismount Backward.* At the peak of the forward swing, swing the legs up towards the rings and straddle the legs as they near the arms. Keep the head backwards. Just before the legs touch the arms release the hands and execute the backward somersault to the feet. A spotter may assist by lifting the performer's shoulders. This stunt is learned first on the still rings.

5. *Regular Flyaway.* This should be tried from still rings first and later attempted with a small swing and finally a large swing. The beat is very similar to that of a straddle dismount backward except that in doing the stunt the legs are between the rings and not in a straddle position. Take a strong beat at the center of the swing and then lift the chest upwards towards the ceiling. Drop the head backwards and at the peak of the upward lift drop the arms and drift over into a high lazy back layout. Do not throw backward too hard or tuck the body as this will cause more than a single back somersault and injuries will result. Have spotter available while learning this stunt.

A high flying flyaway at Muscle Beach, California

CHAPTER 11

Women's Free Exercise

FREE EXERCISE for women is very similar to the men's event in that the performer works on the floor or a thin pad for a maximum time of a minute and a half within a square area; the dimensions of 12 meters (39.33 feet). The women's activity differs from the men's primarily in the composition of the routine in that the women use more movements of the ballet type whereas the men use more power moves. Other than this, the events are carried on in a similar manner. Starting within the prescribed area, the routine generally begins with an opening sequence of tumbling followed by the body of the routine consisting of ballet jumps, turns, spins, balancing and agility movements, and finally finishing with a tumbling sequence. A great amount of inventiveness and artistic thinking can be displayed throughout the free exercise routine for women. It is one of the most flexible events in women's competition.

VALUES

The specific values of working free exercise are:

1. Free exercise develops an appreciation for rhythm and timing.
2. The event will develop coordination and balance to a high degree.

3. A sense for creating will be developed through repeated attempts at composing a fine artistic exercise.
4. Strength and endurance is developed through the hard workouts necessary for the accomplishment of the final routine.

ORGANIZATION

Because of the great similarity between free exercise for men and for women, the organization for instructional purposes is very similar. To avoid lengthy duplication of words, the reader is asked to refer to Chapter 5 on free exercise for men for this aspect of the activity. A few items will be mentioned here as reminders.

Many of the stunts done in free exercise for women should be tried first on a tumbling mat. Later they may be transferred to the floor. It is also highly recommended that a spotter be used while learning some of the more difficult stunts such as valdez, walkovers, backbends, yogi handstands, and so on.

In composing a routine it is suggested that some of the individual stunts or movements be learned thoroughly first and then molded into a neat fundamental exercise. This will give the performer a feeling for the event and later as more difficult stunts are learned they may be inserted at the performer's discretion. Routines should make use of the entire body and include movements and jumps which are full of expression, elegance, individuality, and originality. Remember that an effort should be made to make the connecting moves harmonious when changing rhythm, style, or pace.

It is further suggested that many of the stunts be done before a mirror or reflecting surface so that grace and fine performance can be cultivated early.

PROGRAM OF INSTRUCTION

As was done in the free exercise chapter for men the stunts or movements that can be done in the women's event will be grouped into four groups: ballet, flexibility, balances, and agility. They appear within these groups in a recommended order of learning.

Ballet Movements

As previously mentioned the women's free exercise routine contains several ballet type movements and with this in

Toe stand

mind the following are a few that may be used.

1. *Toe Stand.* Start from a standing position and then rise up on the toes extending the arms to the side palms down. Then drop down to a full standing position with the arms at your sides.

2. *Body Wave.* From a standing position with the hands at the side bend slightly forward and bring the arms

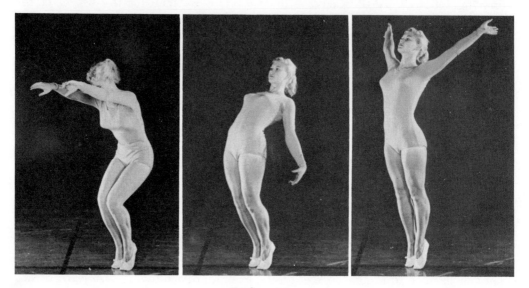

Body wave

backward and upward in a graceful manner. The body executes a facsimile of a waving motion and then returns to the starting position again.

3. *Ballet Touch.* With one foot ahead of the other the performer from a standing position gracefully leans forward to touch the forward foot with one hand. This is often used as a transitional movement from one stunt to another.

4. *Pirouette.* A pirouette is a full turn over a fixed axis on one foot (the ball of the foot) and while the body rotates the head remains looking at the starting point as long as possible. When it no longer can be held in this position the head turns quickly around to face starting point again. Two or more are usually executed. Pirouettes demand supreme control and balance and can be done slow or fast.

5. *Spiral.* From a trunk bending position with flexed knees, little steps are taken to turn in place while arms and body move to one side in a winding motion to toe stand and stretched body. Usually a full turn.

6. *Body Sweep.* This is another ballet type movement and is done as pictured

Stag leap

in that a graceful sweep of the body is executed by swinging one arm forward with the weight on the other arm and knee, keeping other leg extended backward.

7. *Stag Leap.* Leap upward and while in the air bring one foot up under the other leg so that the foot almost touches the knee. The hands are raised at the sides for lift and balance during this leap.

Flexibility Stunts

Just a few of the many stunts that belong in the flexibility group are as follows:

1. *Splits.* This as implied simply means the performer drops downward from a standing position into a neat split. The hands may be raised outward from the shoulders and held in a graceful position.

2. *Straddle Lean.* This consists of doing a straddle stand and dropping downward into a wide front split and then leaning forward until the chest touches the floor.

Body sweep

Straddle lean

Needle scale

Back walkover

3. *Needle Scale.* This stunt starts with the performer leaning forward into a front scale and then continuing downward so the forehead touches the shin of the supporting leg with the other leg elevated directly overhead. This takes extreme flexibility and must be practiced diligently before accomplishing.

4. *Supine Arch Up.* From a supine position on the floor simply elevate the back upward from the floor sliding the hands from a position near the hips backward to a support position.

5. *Back Walkover.* From a standing position bend backward until the hands touch the floor and then kick one leg up and over followed by the other to finish in a standing position again. Be sure to have a spotter during the learning stages of this stunt.

6. *One Leg Balance.* From a standing position, raise one leg to the side as high as you can, grasp its instep with one hand while you gracefully sweep the other arm straight up, palm facing in.

One leg balance

Supine arch up

Front scale

Front walkover

7. *Front Walkover.* Start from a standing position and lean forward placing the hands on the mat or floor ahead of the feet as if going into a handstand. Continue the feet on over to the floor again and land on one foot and then lift the hands off the floor and bring the other foot to the floor. Again a spotter is essential while first learning this stunt.

Balance Movements

This division indicates the stunts that require mainly a balancing technique such as handstand and so on. Some of the stunts that might be included will be discussed.

1. *Arabesque.* From a standing position raise one arm upward and lift one foot off the floor. Hold this position in a graceful manner.

2. *Front Scale.* This could be classed in the ballet type or flexibility groups but it truly is a balancing type of position in that the stunt consists of standing on one foot with the other leg raised to a height parallel to the floor or higher with the forward part of the body lowered to a position parallel to the floor. The arms may be held outward from the shoulders in a graceful manner or one arm may be raised straight ahead with the other along side the body. The head is up with the back arched and the

Arabesque

Balance seat

141

leg fairly straight with the toes pointed.

3. *Balance Seat (V Seat).* This indicates a stunt which consists of simply sitting on the floor with the legs together, elevated to make a "V" with the trunk. The hands may be either on the floor behind the performer or raised outward from the shoulders.

4. *Hand Balance.* The techniques of doing a hand balance are thoroughly covered in Chapter 4, and therefore it will simply be pointed out that the hand balance may be used a few times throughout a free exercise routine. Many different methods of moving into the hand balance position can be left to the imagination of the performer. Simple presses, straight kick up, back bend or cartwheel into hand balance are some suggested methods.

5. *Yogi Hand Balance.* As pictured this consists of holding a hand balance in an unusual position of the body. The hips are forward with the legs back and the head is lifted so that the entire stunt looks fascinating and challenging. One of the easiest methods of moving into the yogi position is to jump into it with the hands on the floor. Push off both feet

and immediately execute the yogi hand balance. While learning, this position may be held for just a second or so and later as skill improves it may be held for several seconds.

Agility Stunts

In this group belong all of the stunts that rely primarily upon the agility of the performer. Tumbling stunts of all sorts, and any other stunts of agile motion, belong in this grouping.

Shoot through

Yogi hand balance

1. *Shoot Through.* From a front leaning rest position with the arms straight flex the hips slightly and then shoot the legs through the arms and finish in a sitting position. The shoot through can be continued on into a back arched position.

2. *Forward Drop.* From a standing position fall forward landing on the hands with the arms straight at first and with a flexing of the arms continue downward to the chest. Lift one leg as the fall is executed so that in the finish position one leg is lifted gracefully and one leg remains on the floor and the upper part of the body is almost resting on the floor with the weight supported by the arms.

Forward drop

Valdez

3. *Valdez.* This is similar to the men's stunt in that the performer sits on the floor with one hand behind the hip and the other arm elevated straight out from the shoulder. One leg is straight and the other is flexed with the foot near the seat. This is as pictured. From this position the elevated arm is thrown overhead and backward and the straight leg is lifted upward. The performer executes a fast back bend motion and finishes either in a handstand position or continues the movement on to a standing position on the feet.

Tumbling Stunts

Rather than list individually some of the tumbling stunts that can be done in women's free exercise it seems advisable to merely name a few and suggest further that the tumbling chapter be consulted as to proper techniques of executing them: rolls, cartwheels, handsprings, headsprings, back handsprings, roundoff, back somersaults, and so on.

CHAPTER 12

Women's Vaulting

THIS EVENT is similar to men's vaulting with one major exception—the vaulting is done over the side of the horse with the pommels removed. The woman performer takes off the beat board on one side of the horse and vaults over with the hands resting mainly on the middle part (saddle) of the horse. Other than that the event is conducted in a similar manner in that a springy type beat board is used, an approach is used by the vaulter, the vaults are similarly named—squat vault, stoop vault, handspring, and so on. Each vault has a difficulty rating and competition involves two vaults.

The measurements of the horse are: 5'10" long and 14" wide, and the height of the horse from the mat to the top of the horse during the vaulting competition is 3'7".

VALUES

The specific values from vaulting are:
1. Develops coordination, timing, and agility.
2. Develops strength and power in the large muscle groups of the entire body.
3. Develops courage and confidence.

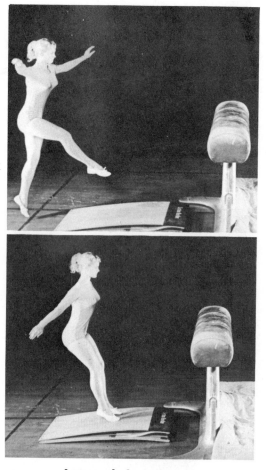

Approach for take-off

ORGANIZATION

To avoid duplication of words it is suggested that reference be made to the lengthy discussion on vaulting in Chapter 7. The same general principles apply for women in learning the correct techniques of springing from the beat board and over the horse.

It is suggested that the horse be set at a comfortable height for beginners. It is further suggested that considerable amount of time be spent on practising the correct fundamentals of taking off the beat board. Be sure to post a spotter on the far side of the horse while practising the vaults and if available, have two spotters with one in front and the other in back of the horse.

PROGRAM OF INSTRUCTION

The following series of vaults is suggested for learning in the order given.

1. *Flank Vault.* As can be seen this consists of passing over the horse with the side of the body closest to the horse. Lean on the supporting arm and keep the body fairly straight while passing over the top of the horse.

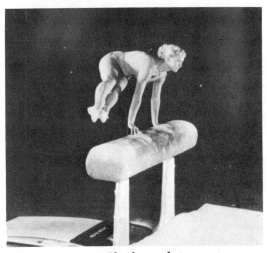

Flank vault

2. *Front Vault.* This is done somewhat like the flank vault only the front part of the body is turned toward the top of the horse while it is passing over it. Allow the feet and legs to lift into the air so that a graceful arch of the body is obtained. Land on the mat with the inside hand resting on the horse for support.

3. *Rear Vault.* This vault entails passing over the horse in a sitting position with the seat of the performer closest to the horse. Upon taking off lift the legs to the side and pass them over the horse in a pike position. Continue on over, change the hands and land on the mat facing the direction of the turn with the inside hand resting on the horse.

4. *Squat Stand—Jump Off Dismount.* After the approach and take-off place the hands on the horse and bring the legs up between the arms and stop in a squat stand position. From this position leap forward to the mat.

Squat stand

5. *Squat Vault.* Take off from the beat board, place the hands on the horse and bring the knees up between the arms. Push hard with the arms and pass over the horse in a squat position and land on the mat on the other side.

Squat vault

6. *Straddle Stand—Forward Jump Off.* Jump to a straddle stand on the horse with the legs on the outside of the arms. From this position straighten up and jump forward to the mat.

7. *Straddle Vault.* After the approach place the hands on the horse and push downward with the arms, and at the same time straddle the legs in order to pass over the horse in a straddle vault position. Keep the head and chest up and try to sail over the horse in a neat straight position rather than a low forward leaning position.

Straddle vault

8. *Thief Vault.* This consists of taking off from one foot and then lifting the other leg upward toward the take-off foot and sailing over the horse in a sitting position. The hands drop to the horse and push strongly as the body continues on over to the mat. The feet are elevated as the hands touch the horse and a neat shoot forward is executed.

9. *Stoop Vault—Bent Hips Ascent.* This vault is similar to the squat vault only the legs are kept straight instead of bent as they are brought through the arms. Also the ascent to the vault itself is done with the body in pike position.

10. *Stoop Vault—Straight Body Ascent.* This is done like the stoop vault above except that the body is extended straight upward at the beginning of the

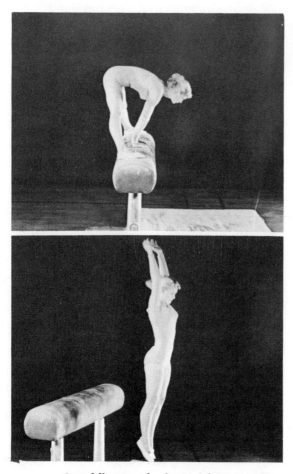

Straddle stand—forward jump off

vault into a partial handstand before the legs are cut through the arms into the stoop vault.

11. *Handspring*. This consists of springing from the board and upward into a handstand position on the horse with the arms straight. From this position continue on over into a handspring or arch over motion to the mat. It is advisable to use a spotter on this stunt, as pictured.

COMPETITIVE VAULTING

The following series of figure drawings (courtesy of the *AAU Gymnastic Handbook*) illustrate the competitive vaults with their degrees of difficulty.

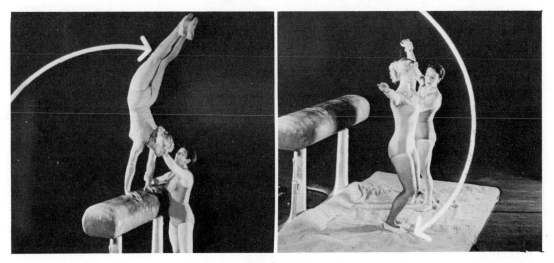

Handspring

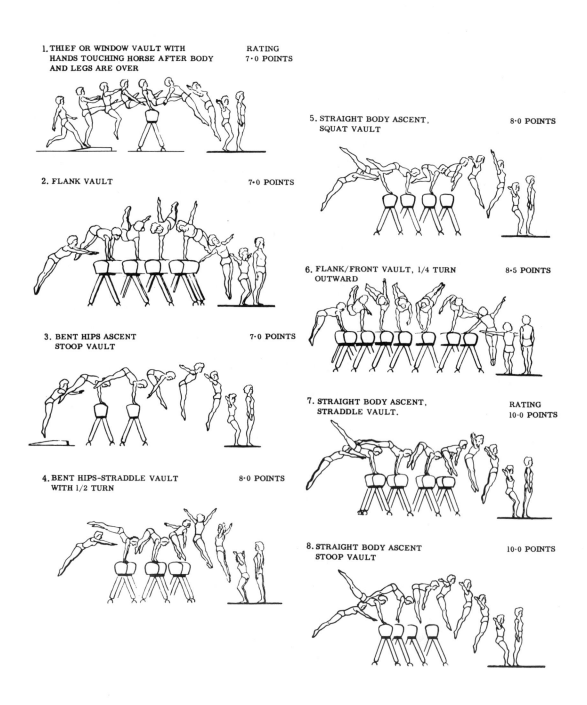

1. THIEF OR WINDOW VAULT WITH
   HANDS TOUCHING HORSE AFTER BODY
   AND LEGS ARE OVER

   RATING
   7·0 POINTS

2. FLANK VAULT

   7·0 POINTS

3. BENT HIPS ASCENT
   STOOP VAULT

   7·0 POINTS

4. BENT HIPS-STRADDLE VAULT
   WITH 1/2 TURN

   8·0 POINTS

5. STRAIGHT BODY ASCENT,
   SQUAT VAULT

   8·0 POINTS

6. FLANK/FRONT VAULT, 1/4 TURN
   OUTWARD

   8·5 POINTS

7. STRAIGHT BODY ASCENT,
   STRADDLE VAULT.

   RATING
   10·0 POINTS

8. STRAIGHT BODY ASCENT
   STOOP VAULT

   10·0 POINTS

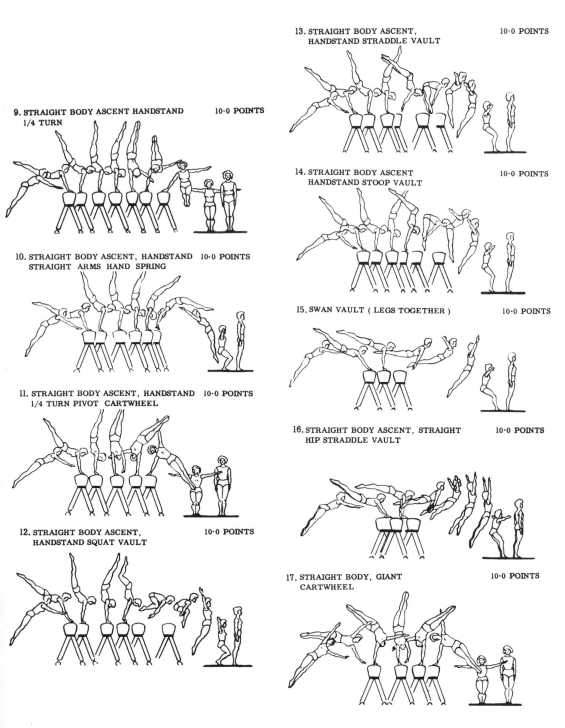

9. STRAIGHT BODY ASCENT HANDSTAND   10·0 POINTS
   1/4 TURN

10. STRAIGHT BODY ASCENT, HANDSTAND   10·0 POINTS
    STRAIGHT ARMS HAND SPRING

11. STRAIGHT BODY ASCENT, HANDSTAND   10·0 POINTS
    1/4 TURN PIVOT CARTWHEEL

12. STRAIGHT BODY ASCENT,   10·0 POINTS
    HANDSTAND SQUAT VAULT

13. STRAIGHT BODY ASCENT,   10·0 POINTS
    HANDSTAND STRADDLE VAULT

14. STRAIGHT BODY ASCENT   10·0 POINTS
    HANDSTAND STOOP VAULT

15. SWAN VAULT (LEGS TOGETHER)   10·0 POINTS

16. STRAIGHT BODY ASCENT, STRAIGHT   10·0 POINTS
    HIP STRADDLE VAULT

17. STRAIGHT BODY, GIANT   10·0 POINTS
    CARTWHEEL

CHAPTER 13

Women's Balance Beam

ASICALLY THE ACTIVITY of balance beam work consists of performing on a beam which is approximately 4″ wide, 16′ long, and resting on tripods about 4′ high. The beat board, which is commonly referred to as a "take-off board," is used for purposes of mounting onto the beam. On this beam gymnasts perform running movements, rolls, held positions, balance positions, and turns all within a 2 minute time limit. This activity presents an exciting challenge to the performer since much control, balance, and courage must be used to maneuver the body through the intricacies of the routine.

Each routine consists of a mount, combinations of movements on the beam, and a dismount. For judging purposes the routines should present a picture of confidence, sureness and control, and elegance and grace. The held positions should be strong and under complete control. This can become a very fascinating and intriguing event.

VALUES

The specific values of working the balance beam are:

1. An accurate sense of balance is gained through work on the balance beam.

2. A feeling of confidence at heights and in a narrow and restricted area is developed.

3. Control and coordination of bodily movements is also developed.

4. Strength is developed throughout the entire body.

ORGANIZATION

Area and Equipment

As can be seen from the dimensions of the balance beam a long and narrow area is required. Of course, several feet on both sides of the beam should be cleared for dismounts and falls. However, the full length of the beam is not needed for individual stunts.

Teaching Methods

It is advisable to practice all of the stunts on a straight line on the gymnasium floor first. The line could be painted on the floor or put on temporarily with tape. Not only is this a good practice method for individuals, but it lends itself handily to the mass method of instruction. This could be handled very much like mass calisthenics.

The next step in learning stunts on the balance beam is to try them on a low balance beam just inches off the floor. When confidence has been established, try the stunts on the high balance beam with an assist from the instructor. Because of the equipment needed, instruction here would be suited best to squads or individuals. Perhaps a system of rotating squads from a line on the floor to the low beam to the high beam would be good to use in a class.

Safety

A few safety rules to be followed in working the balance beam are:

1. Mats should be used on the floor under and at the sides of the high balance beam to provide a soft landing place.

2. Progression in the use of equipment as mentioned above.

3. Learn the stunts in a progressive order so that the proper lead-up activities will be included.

4. Use spotters particularly on the high beam. One spotter on each side of the beam is preferable.

PROGRAM OF INSTRUCTION

Mounts

1. *Straight Arm Support Mount.* Start from a stand or take two or three running steps forward and after a double foot take-off, place the hands on the top of the beam shoulder width apart and jump up to a straight arm support position with the arms straight and the thighs resting on the beam. Hold the head up and arch the body, pointing the toes.

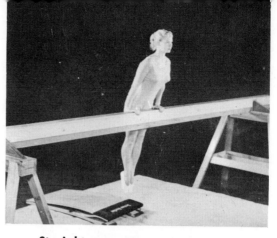

Straight arm support mount

2. *Crotch Seat Mount.* Jump to a straight arm support position and then swing the left leg over the beam with a quarter turn right of the body. The right leg remains on the approach side of the beam and the left leg then swings down and the performer assumes a crotch seat position with the hands on the beam in back of the body.

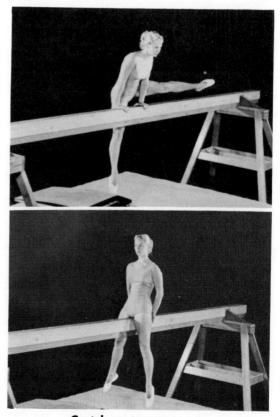

Crotch seat mount

3. *Wolf Vault Mount.* Jump into a straight arm support position bringing one leg in a squat position between the arms and the other leg in a straight extended position to the side and outside of the arms.

Wolf vault mount

4. *Squat Mount.* Similar to Wolf Vault Mount except that both legs are pulled up between the arms and the feet are placed on the beam between the hands.

Squat mount

5. *Straddle Mount.* Jump to a straight arm support position and at the same time spread the legs and place the feet on the beam on the outside of the hands to a straddle support position. Be sure to have a spotter on the opposite side of the beam while trying this stunt for the first few times.

Straddle mount

6. *One Knee Mount.* Jump to a straight arm support position placing one knee on the beam and assuming a kneeling position with the hands supporting the body on the outside of the knee with the other leg stretched backwards.

One knee mount

7. *Chest Balance Mount.* With the hands on the topside of the beam jump

upward into a pike position bending the arms so that the chest faintly touches the beam. Continue the lifting of the legs up and over the head and finally reach the chest balance position. Remember the weight of the body is continuously on the hands and not the chest. Allow the feet to rise slowly and, with sureness of grip, balance the body in a bent arm hand balance with the toes pointed, body arched, head up, and so on.

width apart. Bring the legs up and over the beam into a backward hip circle movement. Finish the stunt in a straight arm support position on the beam.

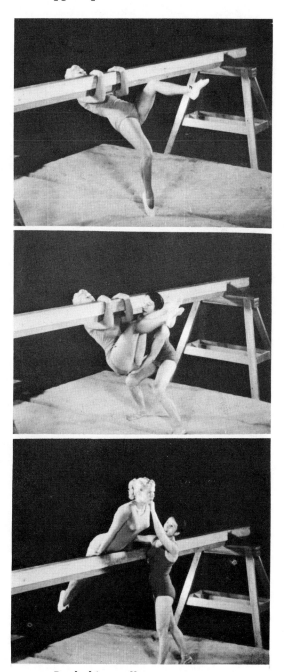

Chest balance mount

8. *Back Hip Pullover Mount.* From a stand bend the knees and grasp the beam with an under grip at shoulder

Back hip pullover mount

9. *Fence Vault Mount.* Approaching from an oblique angle with the beat board placed almost parallel to the beam, leap into a thief vault movement, passing over the beam and landing in a side seat position.

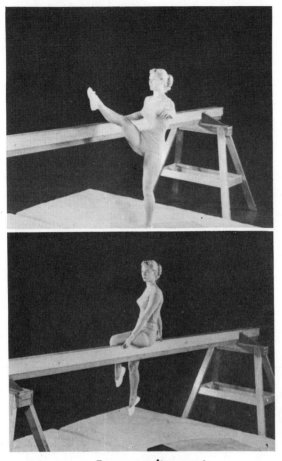

Fence vault mount

Movements on Beam

Using any of the above described mounts the performer is assured of a means of reaching the top side of the beam. Then, after control and balance is secured, the performer may execute several different moves or combinations of movements. Some of these are described.

1. *Walk on Beam.* Walking on the beam should be practiced until it becomes as natural as on the ground. Begin by simply walking forward and backward and then progress to taking a small dip of the knee with each step; allow the free foot to drop slightly below the beam on each dip. The arms are always swung gracefully and freely as the performer moves along the beam. Needless to say the body should be kept straight with the posture good at all times.

2. *Runs on Beam.* After learning the art of walking on the beam, small running steps may be taken. Start first by using exceedingly small steps in the running motion. Later, as skill improves, the steps may be lengthened.

3. *Jumps on Beam.* Jumps have several different methods of execution. A performer can jump or leap from a run or from a dip position. In a squat position with one foot in front of the other, the arms are swung upward and the legs are extended and at the end of the straightening process a leap is executed with an interchange of position of the feet.

Jumps on beam

4. *Turns on Beam.* There are many varieties of turns. One of the easiest is simply to pivot while standing on the beam. With one foot ahead of the other, raise up on the balls of the feet and turn the body 180° and then lower the feet to a walking or standing position.

Turns on beam

A pirouette turn may be done on one foot and can consist of a complete turn or simply a half turn. The arms are held overhead for balance and the body rotates around on the forward part of the supporting foot. Upon completion of the turn the free leg drops immediately to

the beam assuring added balance and support. The pirouette turn can be done either left or right and is thus called an Inward or Outward Pirouette.

5. *Balance Seat* (*V seat*). This stunt is the same as the one described in Chapter 11, except that the hands should remain on the beam behind the body.

Balance seat

6. *Front Scale.* This stunt consists of standing on one leg with the other leg elevated to a position parallel to the beam and the upper body bent forward to a similar position parallel to the beam.

Pirouette

Front scale

The body should have an elegant arch and the raised leg should be straight with the toes pointed. The arms should be extended from the side in a graceful manner with the head up and eyes looking toward the end of the beam. Side scales are variations of this, done to the side instead of forward.

Knee scale

7. *Knee Scale.* Start from a kneeling position with one knee behind the other. Lean forward lifting the back leg into the air and with arms straight place the hands on the beam in front of you.

8. *One Leg Squat.* From a standing position lower into a full squat position on one leg with the other leg lifted parallel to the beam.

One leg squat

9. *Straddle Hold.* From a straddle stand, balance the weight on the hands between the legs, and lower your feet forward, supporting yourself with straight arms.

Straddle hold

10. *Splits.* Forward or side splits can be done on the balance beam. Be sure these are done successfully on the floor before attempting on the balance beam.

11. *Back Arch.* Start this stunt from a supine position on the beam with the hands back over the head grasping the sides of the beam and the legs close together on the top of the beam. Slide the feet in towards the body and then push with the arms and legs and force an arch in the body. This should be done slowly at first without exaggerating the arch and with a spotter's assistance.

12. *Back Shoulder Roll.* This is started from a lying position on the beam. Place the hands on the beam over the head and grip under the beam with the fingers. Place the head on one side of the beam and pull the body over into a backward roll. The knees are pulled up toward the chest and on over the body. The weight of the body is supported on the one shoulder. The legs continue on over toward the beam and one knee is placed on the top of the beam on the completion of the backward shoulder

roll. From this position the performer may continue on to the feet or go into a kneeling scale, or various other movements.

this position the performer may swing the legs downward on each side of the beam to a crotch seat or other such movements.

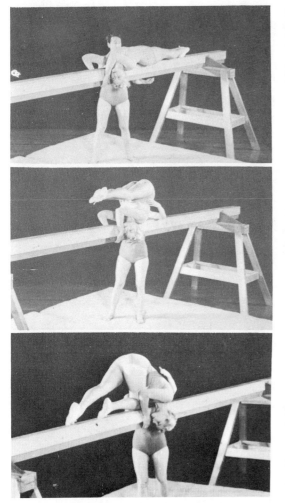

Back shoulder roll

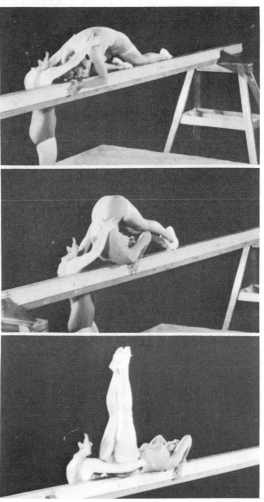

Forward roll

13. *Forward Shoulder Roll.* Start this stunt from a kneeling position. Place the head and one shoulder on one side of the beam with the hands gripping the beam so that the fingers circle the underside of the beam. Slowly move the hips up and into the forward roll motion. Continue the roll so the body finishes in a full lying position on the beam. From

14. *Shoulder Balance.* Start this from a kneeling position. Place one shoulder on the beam. The hands grip the underside of the beam. Slowly lift the hips upward by pushing gently with the legs. Finally lift both legs up and over the head and assume a shoulder balance on the beam. A spotter should assist the performer throughout this stunt.

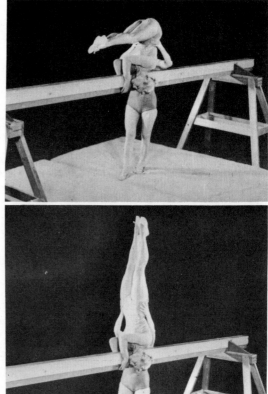

Cartwheel to hand balance **Shoulder balance**

15. *Cartwheel to Hand Balance.* Basically this consists of simply doing a cartwheel into the hand balance position. This movement should be practiced many times on the floor before attempting it on the balance beam. Start with the legs in a straddle position with the body turned slightly ready to lean into the cartwheel. Place one hand on the beam and at the same time kick the back leg upward towards the hand balance position. Then place the other hand on the beam into a good hand balance position and bring the other leg upward to join the first leg and move the entire body into a solid hand balance position. Be sure to work with a spotter or two at all times while first learning this stunt.

16. *English Hand Balance.* This is a hand balance facing the length of the beam with the hands close together on each side of the beam. Start from a standing position and then bend forward and place the hands on the beam with the fingers down the sides and the thumbs on top almost touching each other. From this position the performer kicks into the English hand balance. Remember to keep the head up, body arched, toes pointed, legs together, and so on.

Dismounts

There are several methods of dismounting neatly to the mat at the end of the routine.

1. *Jump Off Dismount.* Probably the easiest and most simple dismount is merely to leap off the beam either at the end or the sides. This should be done gracefully and the landing should be soft and effortless. More difficulty may be added to this type of dismount by executing a straddle position while in the air with hands touching the toes, or finishing with a half twist or even assuming a stag jump position while in the air.

2. *Side Seat Dismount.* From a side seat position in the middle of the beam lean forward and place the right hand on the top side of the beam. Swing the outside leg backward and at the same time lift the body from the beam. Move the body slightly to the side and drop to the mat.

3. *Front Vault Dismount.* From a front leaning rest position resting on the toes and straight arms, kick one leg upward followed by the other and at the same time move body slightly to the side. Drop to the mats.

Side seat dismount

Front vault dismount

4. *English Hand Balance Dismount.* From a standing position swing the arms down and place the hands on the beam in an English Hand Balance Position. Continue the feet upward into a partial hand balance. From this position simply move the body slightly to one side and execute a Front Vault Dismount to the mats.

English hand balance dismount

5. *Cartwheel.* Near the end of the beam lean sideward and execute a cartwheel on the end of the beam and continue off the end of the beam to the mat. Be sure to lengthen the cartwheel so the landing is done squarely to the feet and not too far over to the side of the body, and so on.

6. *Shoulder Balance Side Dismount.* From a shoulder balance dismount to the mat by executing a cartwheel type of movement sideward off the shoulder to the side opposite from the head. Keep the hand on the near side of the beam constantly in contact with the beam to provide support and balance upon landing on the mat.

7. *Handstand Arch Over.* From a handstand position execute an arch over to the mat. Have a spotter present to prevent falling backwards toward the beam.

8. *Hand Balance Squat Through.* From a hand balance in the middle of the beam execute a squat through to the mats.

9. *Handspring.* Stand approximately in the middle of the beam and lean forward and place the hands on the beam and execute a front handspring off the beam to the mat. The handspring is done in general direction of the beam.

CHAPTER 14

Women's Even and Uneven Parallel Bars

THE EVEN PARALLEL BARS is an event which has been with the women's gymnastic field for a good many years, while the uneven bars were not introduced to the competitive world until the 14th Summer Olympic Games in Helsinki in 1952. By that time the International Federation of Women's Gymnastics had realized the great possibilities of performing many more varied stunts on the uneven bars, and also the preponderance of support work involved in the even parallel bars. The change to uneven parallel bars that they recommended has since been accepted in Olympic, International, and National Competition.

Even though greater emphasis is now placed on the uneven bars in women's competition there still exists a fine place for the even parallel bars in the women's physical education field. The dimensions of the parallel bars are similar to those of the men's which have previously been covered. The measurements of the uneven bars are: Height of the high bar from the floor to the top of the bar is approximately 7' 6" and the height of

the low bar is approximately 5'. The width of the inside measurements is between 16½" and 18". As in the balance beam event it is permissible to use a beat board for mounting purposes.

Mounting uneven bars from beat board

VALUES

The specific values received from working on the even and uneven parallel bars are:

1. Develops strength and endurance in the arms and the upper body.

2. Develops confidence in one's ability to control the body while maneuvering through stunts of moderate difficulty at substantial height.

3. Develops a sense of balance and timing while working from one bar to the other and while performing balancing stunts on one bar aided by the other.

ORGANIZATION

The organization of a class for instructional purposes in women's parallel bars is similar to that of men's parallel bars which is treated in an earlier chapter. Reference should be made to that chapter for this information. It might be advisable to teach stunts on the even parallel bars before proceeding to the unevens. Not only will the stunts be a little easier but the performer will gain confidence which will help her when starting the uneven bars.

Because some of the stunts on the uneven parallel bars are similar to horizontal bar stunts, a low horizontal bar might be helpful to supplement the instruction. The horizontal bar lowered at a comfortable height will provide for easier learning and safer spotting. The spotter should spot stunts done on the higher bar from a position underneath that bar as is done on the horizontal bar. It is preferable that while learning routines two spotters be used in order to cover safely the variety of stunts. The even parallel bars should be lowered to their lowest height during the early learning phase. Be sure to progress slowly and surely so that the fundamental movements are mastered.

PROGRAM OF INSTRUCTION

Stunts will be presented here for both the even and uneven parallel bars. Only a few will be given for the former since more emphasis is now placed on the latter. For more stunts that can be done on even bars consult the chapter on men's parallel bars.

Even Parallel Bars

1. *Straight Arm Support.* This is a position for many of the stunts that are done on the parallel bars. It consists of jumping upward into a straight arm support position either on the ends of the bar or in the middle. Keep the arms straight, head up, back arched, and toes pointed. One may travel the length of the bars in this position by merely shifting the weight from hand to hand.

Straight arm support

2. *Straddle Seat.* Start from an approach stance and jump forward supporting the body with the arms. Swing the legs between the bars and up above the bars. When the legs reach the height of the bars separate them in a straddle position and place them on the bars and finish in a straddle seat position with the hands on the bars behind the back. One may also travel the length of the bars in a straddle seat travel by placing the hands on the bars in front of the legs, leaning forward and swinging the legs

backward and then forward between the bars to another straddle seat.

Straddle seat

3. *Side Seat (Riding Seat)*. From a straight arm support position swing forward and pass both legs up and over one of the bars. Finish in a neat side seat position with the hands behind the body on each of the bars. A rhythmical series of side seats may be performed by swinging the legs upward into the side seat from a straight arm support position and then back again.

Riding seat

4. *Forward Roll*. Start from a straddle seat position and then bend forward placing the hands on the bars in front of the body and start a forward roll motion. Roll over on the upper arms and when about half way over place the hands behind the back with fingers almost touching and form a bridge on which the body continues to roll over into a straddle seat position again. Use a spotter on this stunt.

Forward roll

5. *Shoulder Balance (Upper Arm Balance)*. Start from a straddle seat position with the hands on the bars in front of the body. Lean forward and place the upper arms on the bar and slowly lift the hips and legs up into the shoulder balance position. Keep the head up and slowly move into a neat shoulder balance with the back arched, legs straight and toes pointed.

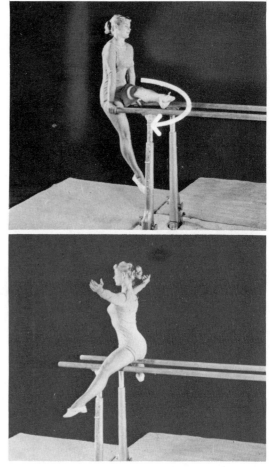

Upper arm balance

6. *Front Leg Cut On to Straddle Seat.* From an approach stance, jump upward to a straight arm support position. At the same time swing the left leg over left bar and continue it over the right bar stopping it short of the right hand. Pivot your body backwards to the right and bring the right leg up and over the left bar to finish in a straddle seat position facing out.

7. *Back Roll to Straddle Seat.* Start in a rear stand approach facing away from the bar. From this stance lift your legs up into an inverted hang and then continue them over towards the bars, circling each around a bar to a position of straddle hook. Continue the backward roll movement using your legs to elevate

Front leg cut on to straddle seat

your body up and on top of the bars into a straddle seat.

8. *Single Leg Cut Off Backward Dismount.* Start from a straight arm support position on the ends of the bars facing the length of the bars. Swing back and forth a couple of times and then upon reaching the peak of the forward swing lift one leg over the bar and backwards towards the mat. Lift the arm so that the leg may pass underneath it and then regrip the bar with the hand after the leg has passed beyond the end. Land in a standing position on the mats with both hands on the bars.

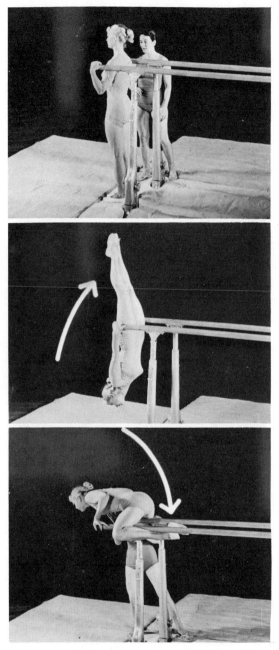

Back roll to straddle seat

9. *Single Leg Cut Off Forward Dismount.* From a straight arm support position facing out away from the bars swing back and forth a couple of times. On the back end of one of the swings lift one leg up and over the bar. Release

the grip on one hand and allow the leg to pass between it and the bar. Continue moving forward and land on the mat in a dismount fashion. Use a spotter on this stunt.

Single leg cut off forward dismount

10. *Rear Vault Dismount.* Swing back and forth a couple of times in a straight arm support position and on the forward end swing both legs up and over the bar. Continue the movement to the side passing over the right bar if the dismount is done to the right side and finish facing the same direction with the right hand free and the left hand holding the bar for support.

Rear vault dismount

11. *Single Leg Flank Dismount.* Start with body in a resting position sideways across the bars with one leg over forward bar and other leaning on rear bar. Swing your back leg up and around the bars and push off the front bar and drop to the mat in a neat landing.

Single leg flank dismount

Uneven Parallel Bars

The stunts that can be done on the uneven parallel bars will be grouped into the following three divisions: mounts, stunts or combinations of movements and dismounts.

Mounts

There are numerous methods of mounting onto the uneven parallel bars and the following material will attempt to cover a few of these:

1. *Mount to Straight Arm Support.* Stand facing the low bar with the hands grasping the bar with a regular grip (fingers over the top with the thumbs underneath). The performer then jumps up toward the bar and finishes in a straight arm support position with the thighs resting on the bar, arms straight, chest and head up, legs straight, and toes pointed.

Straight arm support

2. *Back Pullover Mount.* Start facing the low bar with the hands grasping the bar in an overgrip. Pull in towards the

Back pullover mount

bar with the arms and lift one leg up and
over the top of the bar, following it immediately with the other. Continue to
pull both legs over the bar. Keep pulling
with the arms and complete the back hip
circle so that the body finishes in a
straight arm support position as in the
mount above.

3. *Cross Seat Mount.* Start by standing
between the bars facing the length with
the right shoulder toward the low bar
and the left toward the high bar. From
this position jump upwards and grasp
the high bar with the left hand and the
low bar with the right hand and then
swing both legs up and over the low bar
to a cross seat position.

**Shoot over low bar from hang on
high bar**

4. *Shoot over Low Bar from Hang on
High Bar.* Start behind the high bar
facing the low bar and after the ap-

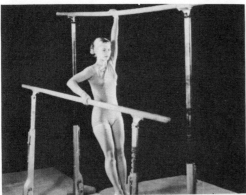

Cross seat mount

proach and take-off grasp the high bar, then swing both legs up and over the low bar and finish in a position with the back of the thighs resting on the low bar and the hands holding the high bar so the body is in a hanging lying position.

5. *Squat Stand Mount.* Start a few feet away from the low bar, after an approach and a double foot take off, place both hands on the bar and lift the knees up toward the chest and place the feet on the bar in a squat position. Upon reaching the squat position immediately rise upward to a straight standing position and grasp the high bar with both hands.

6. *Single Leg Swing-Up.* Start facing the low bar with the hands resting shoulder width apart on the top of the bar. Jump into the air and bring one leg into a tuck position between the arms and quickly circle the bar with this leg. Allow the body to swing down and under the bar swinging on the hock of the one leg supporting part of the weight with the two arms. On the return swing whip the free leg downward forcefully and pull with the arms. Continue the circle so the body rides up to the top

Single leg swing up

of the bar with one leg in front and the other behind and the hands supporting the body.

7. *Flank Mount (Low Bar).* Face the low bar and after a few running steps toward it and a double foot take-off place both hands on the low bar and execute a right flank movement over the low bar and then immediately release the left hand and grasp the high bar. Keep right hand on low bar. Finish in a side seat position on the low bar facing toward the high bar.

8. *Flank with Half Twist.* Start behind the high bar facing the low bar. After the run and double foot take-off grasp the high bar and lift both legs up to the right and execute a flank movement over the low bar. When the legs pass over the low bar then turn half way in toward the low bar and finish with the hips resting on the low bar with both hands grasping the high bar.

Dismounts

Since much of the elementary work on the uneven bars might consist of mounting and immediately dismounting it may be feasible to concentrate at this time on the various methods of dismounting from the bars.

1. *Cast off Low Bar with Quarter Twist.* This is done from a straight arm support position on the low bar facing the high bar. Allow the feet to swing under the bar slightly and then force them backward. As the legs lift off the bar, push with the arms, turn the body a quarter turn and simply drop to the mat in a standing position a few inches away from the bar with the left side closest to the bar and the left hand continuing to hold for support purposes.

Cast off low bar with a quarter twist

2. *Single Leg Flank Vault Dismount* (*Low Bar*). Start in a crotch seat position with the left leg in front and the right leg behind the low bar with the back toward the high bar. The left hand is in an undergrip on the low bar and the right hand is in an overgrip on the high bar. Swing the right leg up and over the right side of the bar. Support the body mostly with the left arm. As the right leg passes over the bar, the right hand releases its grip and the body is stretched toward the right and continues downward to the mats. Land on the mat with the left hand still on the bar and the left side of the bar closest to the bar.

Single leg flank vault dismount

3. *L Position Shoot Off Dismount.* From a sitting position on the low bar with the back toward the high bar lift the feet into the air and cast the body

away from the bar. Push with the hands and then land on the feet a few feet away from the low bar.

4. *Rear Vault with Quarter Turn Dismount.* Start between the bars grasping the low bar and high bar as you lean forward. Swing your legs up and over the low bar. Push off high bar, turning your body to an L seat position over the low bar. Continue the motion into the dismount to the feet.

5. *Forward Roll Off High Bar.* Stand on the low bar facing high bar. Lean into the high bar placing the abdomen on the bar and the hands in reverse grip position. Continue to roll on over the top of the bar and down to a straight hang position. Then with a small whip of the legs snap outward to the mat.

6. *Underswing Dismount (Low Bar).* Start in a straight arm support position on the low bar with the back toward the high bar. Swing the legs slightly backward and then in towards the bar. Start a back hip circle movement but at the bottom of the swing shoot the feet up and away from the bar. Pull with the arms and continue the shoot to the mat so as to land in a standing position a few feet away from the low bar. A graceful arch of the body while shooting away from the bar makes this an easy yet pleasant dismount.

7. *Flank Vault (Low Bar).* Start this in a straight arm support position on the low bar with the back towards the high bar. Bring the legs up and over the right side of the bar and execute a flank vault over this bar. Land on the mat with the back towards the low bar.

8. *Underswing Dismount from High Bar.* Stand on the low bar facing the

Rear vault with quarter turn dismount

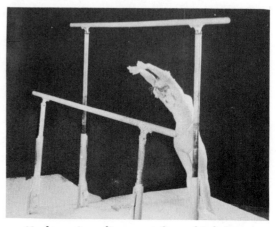

Underswing dismount from high bar

high bar and the hands resting on top of the high bar. Jump into a partial pike position and swing the legs under and upwards under the high bar. Continue the swing into an underswing dismount. This is similar to the underswing on the low bar but with the added height it becomes an attractive dismount.

9. *Squat Through Dismount.* Start from a straight arm support position on the low bar. Lift the legs upward and immediately squat the legs through the arms and pass the feet over the bar. Continue the movement toward the mat and land in a standing position on the mats with the back toward the bar. This same dismount can be done with the legs straight and thus it becomes a stoop vault dismount, or the legs can be in a straddle position and thus it is a straddle dismount.

10. *Front Vault from High Bar over Low Bar.* From a front lying position on the high bar lean forward and downward toward the low bar. Grasp the low bar with a mixed grip with the left hand in an undergrip and the right hand in an overgrip. When the hands are securely grasping the low bar then with the aid of the high bar whip the legs out and over the low bar. Allow the body to pass over the low bar in a front vault position and land on the mat on the other side of the low bar. Continue to hold onto the low bar with the left hand.

Stunts or Combinations

1. *Right Leg over Bar.* This stunt is generally done after a single knee swing up to a support position. The left leg is in front and the right leg behind (scissors fashion). Lift the right leg up and over the right side of the bar. As the leg passes over the bar lift the right hand and then grasp the high bar. Finish in a side seat position with the left

hand grasping the low bar and the right hand the high bar.

2. *Crotch Seat.* From a straight arm support position on the inside of the low bar bring the right leg up and over the right side of the bar. Continue the leg over the bar and finish the stunt in a crotch seat position with the left hand on the high bar and the right hand on the low bar.

Crotch seat

3. *Seat Balance.* From a side seat position or a straddle seat position bring right leg up onto the bar, and extend the left leg as in the V seat position. Aid the balance by holding the high bar with the left hand and the low bar with the right hand behind the back.

Seat balance

4. *One Leg Squat.* Start with the right foot on the low bar with the body in a completely squat position with the left

One leg squat

One leg squat to scale

hand on the top bar and the right hand on the low bar in front of the foot. From here raise upward into a scale position with the left leg raised back in a scale position and the right hand lifted straight forward. Hold this scale position.

5. *Squat Stand on Low Bar, Swing up to Front Support on High Bar.* Start with the right foot on the low bar and the left hand on the high bar. Swing the left leg up and over the high bar. Bring the right leg over also and finish in a front support position with the hands on the high bar on each side of the body.

Squat stand on low bar, swing up to front support on high bar

6. *Swan Support.* From a straight arm support position on high bar, hold the arms straight out at the sides and execute a swan arch position.

Swan support

7. *Kick Off Low Bar to High Bar Support.* Start from a hanging position on the high bar and then swing slightly forward and place one foot on the low bar. On the return swing push the foot, whip the other leg down and pull the body up and over the top bar. Continue the movement so that the body ends in a straight arm support position on the high bar. This can be done with both feet on the bar instead of just one.

8. *Thigh Rest.* From a front rest position on the high bar drop downward and grasp the low bar with the hands, arms straight. Lift the legs so that the body is arched and resting on the hands and thighs.

Thigh rest

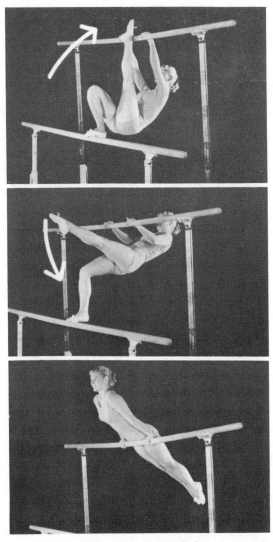

Kick off low bar to high bar support

9. *Double Leg Bounce to Straight Arm Support.* Start from a hanging position on the high bar. Lift both legs over the right side of the low bar and allow them to drop forcefully on the bar, and with an effect of a rebound bring the legs up and over the high bar. Pull hard with the arms and continue the movement into a back hip pullover on the high bar. Finish in a straight arm support position.

Double leg bounce to straight arm support

10. *Arch Back.* Hang on the knees on the high bar facing low bar and reach backward towards the low bar with the hands. Grasp the low bar and pull the body up and over the bar continuing to hang on the high bar with the knees. Finish in an arched position with the arms straight from the low bar and the back of the legs resting on the high bar.

11. *Single Knee Circle Backward.* After executing a single knee swing up on the low bar facing the high bar with the left leg in front and the right leg behind, shift the body backward and at the same time allow the hock of the left leg to hook onto the low bar. Swing the right leg downward and under the bar.

Arch back

Continue this back knee circle movement under the bar and on over the other side of the bar. Pull with the arms near the completion of the stunt and finish in the original starting position with the left leg forward and the right leg behind. The single knee circle may be done forward also.

12. *Straddle Seat.* From a single leg straddle position bring the other leg up and over into a straddle seat with the hands supporting the body between the legs.

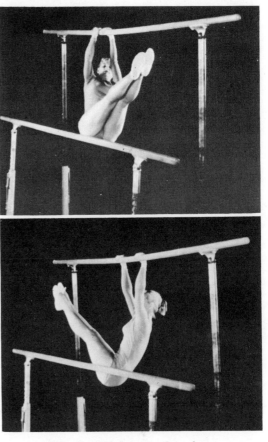

Double leg circle over low bar

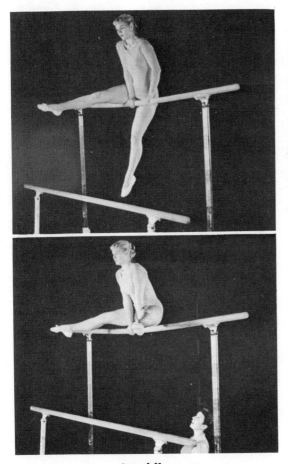

Straddle seat

13. *Double Leg Circle over Low Bar.* Start from a hanging position on the high bar. Swing the legs up and over the low bar without touching it. Continue the swing back to the starting position.

14. *Back Hip Circle.* Start from a straight arm support position on the low bar. Lift the legs up in back and then allow them to swing downward toward the bar. Just as they reach the bar swing the hips downward and under the bar pulling with the arms. Pike the body slightly as the backward hip circle continues around the bar. Be sure to shift the wrists so that at the end of it they are in a support position again. Continue the backward movement until the body finishes in a straight arm support position.

15. *Half Turn Swing on High Bar to Back Hip Circle on Low Bar.* Start by sitting on the low bar facing the high

Back hip circle

Half turn swing on high bar to back hip circle on low bar

bar. Grasp the high bar with the hands in a mixed grip, the left hand in an overgrip and the right hand in an undergrip. Swing the legs under the low bar slightly and then swing them forward away from the low bar. The body is then supported by the arms in a hanging position. At the peak of the forward swing execute a half turn to the left and continue the body toward the low bar. Upon contacting the low bar release the hands from the high bar and quickly grasp the low bar and execute a backward hip circle.

16. *Back Hip Pullover on High Bar.* Start in a standing position on the low

bar with the hands in an overgrip on the high bar. Push off the feet and pull with the arms and pass the legs under and over and around the high bar in a back hip circle movement. Continue the hip circle until the body reaches the straight arm support position.

17. *Straddle Leg Swing-Up to a Hang Lying on Low Bar.* Start by standing underneath the high bar facing the low bar. Grasp the low bar and glide the legs under the bar on the forward part of the swing. On the return swing quickly bring the legs up and on the outside of the arms shoot them over the bar. When the body reaches a position

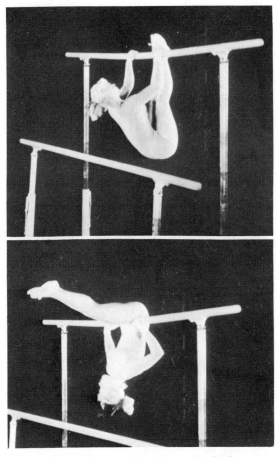

Back hip pullover on high bar **Half turn jump low bar to high bar**

of half sitting on the low bar then reach upwards and grasp the high bar. Finish in a lying position across the low bar with the hands grasping the high bar and arms supporting the upper body.

18. *Half Turn Jump from Low Bar to High Bar.* From a front support position on the low bar swing the legs underneath the bar slightly. Then whip them backwards and at the same time push with the hands executing a half turn to the left. Finish by grasping the high bar with both hands in a hanging position. Be sure to use a spotter in learning this stunt.

19. *Double Knee Hang to a Side Hand*

Balance on Low Bar. From a double knee hang on the high bar facing the low bar reach forward and grasp the low bar with both hands in an overgrip. Pull the body over the low bar with the arms and place one foot on the high bar. Slowly lift the other leg off the bar and gently remove the foot off the bar so that a free hand balance on the low bar is held. Generally a drop down into a backward hip circle is executed from this position.

20. *Side Cross Hand Balance.* From a front lying position on the high bar lean forward toward the low bar. The left hand is on the high bar in an undergrip

and as the body is lowered downward, the right hand is placed in an overgrip on the low bar. Turn the body slightly to the left and slowly press the body away from the high bar so that a cross hand balance may be executed. Keep the right arm straight and the left arm bent. Keep the body close to the high bar throughout the learning phases of this stunt. Later as proficiency develops a flag handstand may be tried, which simply places the body away from the bars with the left arm straight as well as the right arm.

Side cross hand balance

21. *Glide Kip.* From a standing position facing outwards with hands on the low bar jump backwards slightly. With the legs straight glide forward with the feet just inches off the mat. Upon reaching the full extension position, pike the body sharply and bring the feet up towards the bar. Kick upward and outward with the legs pulling strongly with the arms and finish in a front support position.

Glide kip

CHAPTER 15

Rope Activities

ROPE ACTIVITIES include such items as rope skipping, jumping, and climbing.

Rope skipping employs a single light leap to each swing of the rope with the rope being swung by the individual doing the skipping. On the other hand, rope jumping refers to the more erratic, jolting movement over the longer rope being swung by two helpers. The term may also refer to jumping over a static rope at various levels or as it wiggles on the ground. Of course, rope climbing refers to the actual climbing of a suspended rope or the stunts done while on such a rope.

VALUES

1. Children of all ages can have a great deal of fun in skipping and jumping since it is such a natural play activity. One can witness this enjoyment among a group of children indulging in normal play on a summer afternoon. It definitely serves as a release for pent-up muscular energy.

2. Rope skipping is fundamentally simple but it can be advanced to a high degree of skill and achievement and is interesting enough to carry over into post school life. Because one can skip rope in a small space and during any free time, it promotes self-enjoyment, thus providing a good medium for recreation and sport expression regardless of the age or sex.

3. The physical benefits derived from rope activities are numerous as can be seen by their heavy use in conditioning programs of boxers and other athletes. Rope skipping exercises such as boxers perform develop agility, motor coordination, and a sense of rhythm and balance. Rope activities also build endurance and stamina and strengthen the skeletal muscles. Rope climbing is especially good for building up the arms, shoulder and chest muscles and developing explosive power. For this reason it is of particular value in training pole vaulters, wrestlers, and gymnasts.

ORGANIZATION

The rope activities of skipping, jumping, and climbing can be very easily added to the physical education program. First of all they are very inexpensive to incorporate into the existing facilities. Only the climbing ropes require a structure, and any substantial beam or ceiling can be used as a point of suspension. The ropes seldom need replacing due to their durability. Rope activities are also economical in space requirements in that a very small storage space is required for the skipping or jumping ropes, and the climbing ropes may be pulled out of the way very easily.

PROGRAM OF INSTRUCTION

Rope Skipping

Sneakers or moccasins are recommended for skipping rope. Shoes may be used but the rope is apt to catch on the heel. If allowance is made for the heel the jump is too high for good skipping form. For exhibition skipping pliable dress shoes with the heel removed and a patch of rubber sole to prevent slipping is recommended. These shoes are light and flexible yet give good support.

A Number 8 or Number 9 sash cord is recommended for use in rope skipping although any rope can be used with varying degrees of success. It should be long enough to be from armpit to armpit as the skipper stands on the center of the rope, or from hip to hip as the skipper stands in a stride position on the rope. For speed skipping, one or two knots in each end will shorten it enough for maximum performance. Some skipping ropes are adjustable through a device within the handles.

Any available space with sufficient headroom can be adapted for skipping rope. However, some surfaces have preference over others. All surfaces should be free of loose dirt and dust.

1. A smooth, hard-packed dirt surface is fair. The people at the rear of the skipper should be cautioned about the stones and dirt picked up and thrown by the rope. Dust will be stirred up and inhaled if the earth is too dry.

2. A hard wooden surface is good if it isn't too slippery and hazardous. Care should be taken to see that the skippers do not overdo so that the muscle attachments become irritated in the legs.

3. A semihard wooden surface is very good because of the "give" that it has. It helps performance and reduces fatigue.

4. Cement, asphalt tile, or marble floors can be used and are more efficient for speed skipping but they are fatiguing and may be injurious to the metatarsal arch and may cause shin-splints. If the surface is rough it retards performance and causes undue wear on the rope.

Rope skipping lends itself very easily to mass instruction. A comfortable distance must be provided between jumpers. The instructor might find it advisable to teach from a small platform two or three feet high. It is also imperative that the instruction start from the simple and progress to the more difficult. The

Rope skipping class

following are some suggestions in handling the entire class.

1. Demonstration of rope skipping can be done by the instructor or by other students during the class period.

2. Class may be divided into squads and instructed by squad leaders.

3. Rope skipping competition in the fundamental skills can be held with emphasis on quality rather than quantity.

4. The use of films on rope skipping will help the teacher instruct students in the fundamental and advanced skills.

5. Make available the current articles on rope activities for added motivation.

The following suggestions may be used to introduce and teach the activity of rope skipping:

1. *Mimetic games* involving jumping, hopping, and skipping. This serves as a warm-up for the activity of skipping rope.

2. *Jumping in response to commands.* The instructor asks the class to hop to a cadence which is called out; it should be varied by the instructor to maintain alertness.

3. *Jumping in response to music.* To develop a sense of timing the instructor may play several records of different rhythms or a piano may be played and the students asked to hop to the beat of the music.

4. *Jumping with an imaginary rope.* Using no rope but allowing the hands to respond as if a rope was present, try skipping this imaginary rope and keeping the following techniques in mind:

    a. Feet, ankles, and knees together.
    b. Head erect, back straight, chest out, and eyes up.
    c. Jump off the floor about one inch.
    d. Each landing must be on the balls of the feet with the knees bent slightly to break the shock of the landing.

    e. The upper arms are close to the sides with the hands eight to ten inches from the thighs.
    f. The hands circumscribe a circle of about five inches in diameter while skipping.

5. *Introduce the rope to the students* and have all of them try skipping the rope independent of each other. Allow the students a sufficient amount of free time to practice on their own the skill of skipping a rope.

6. *Mass skipping.* Have all the students start with the rope behind them and do five to ten forward consecutive skips. They should start on a given command and a cadence kept while the entire class executes the specified number of skips. Progress to series of 20 skips or more.

7. *Skip rope backwards.* Have the entire class first try skipping backwards with an imaginary rope and after the "feel" has been accomplished then attempt two or three skips with the rope. Start with the rope in front and lift it over the head into the backward spin. Start this on a given command and execute a specified number of backward skips.

8. *Skip forward or backward at a faster pace* than in first learning the skill. This improves confidence and results in skilled performers.

9. *Skip the rope forward while hopping on one leg.* Try alternating the foot after so many hops on one foot followed by same number on the other foot.

10. *Alternating spreads.* Spread the legs sidewards on every other jump. The legs are spread apart on one jump and brought together on the second.

11. *Consecutive spreads.* This is done as in 10 except the legs are brought together on each downward swing of the rope and spread apart to land.

12. *Leg flings.* One leg is flung sideward or forward alternately as the rope passes under the feet and brought together as it descends for the next jump.

13. *Sideward and forward jumps.* Both legs are lifted sideward or forward as the rope passes under the feet.

14. *Alternate to the sides.* Jump rope forward and on every other circle of the rope allow it to pass by the side of the body instead of under the feet. Thus it will pass first under the feet then to the right side of the body then under the feet then to the left side of the body, and so on.

15. *Crisscross—forward and backward.* As the rope descends the arms are crossed at the elbows forming a loop with the rope large enough for the performer to skip through. The arms are uncrossed on the second skip.

16. *Double jump—forward and backward.* As the rope descends, an extra snap of the wrist gives the rope more speed and it passes under the feet twice with but one jump.

17. *Partner skipping.* Two students skipping in the same rope with one of them turning the rope.

18. *Combinations.* Any of the above suggested stunts in rope skipping can be combined into clever and stimulating routines. It is important to start with the simple routines and progress to the more difficult.

Competition. Rope skipping competition may be held to determine the champion of each room, grade, sex, or school. Some suggested items to be used for testing or competition are as follows:

1. A set number of consecutive forward skips

2. A set number of consecutive backward skips

3. A set number of consecutive forward alternate to the sides (front, left side, front, right side, etc.)

4. Same as 3 except backwards

5. A set number of consecutive forward skips on one foot

6. A set number of consecutive backward skips on one foot

7. A set number of consecutive forward crisscrosses

8. Same as 7 except backwards

9. A set number of consecutive forward double jumps

10. Same as 9 except backwards

11. Highest number of consecutive skips in 30 seconds (may use any of the above mentioned stunts for this)

12. Time required for 50 skips

13. Relay contests may be used with individuals running in a skipping rope.

Rope Jumping

For variety and additional stimulation the class may divide into small groups and attempt some rope jumping. Rope jumping consists of two persons swinging the rope while a third person jumps it. The rope should be approximately 10′ long, and heavy enough to describe the circle without losing its tautness. The rope should be swung at a clean brisk pace. Some suggested rope jumping skills include:

Entering a turning rope. The student should place himself near one of the twirlers and on the side where the rope circles downward toward the floor. As soon as the rope passes him and strikes the floor the student jumps into the area of the skipping. The rope in the meantime continues on up and over into another circle and on the down swing the student proceeds to jump and continues thereon.

Exit from turning rope. The exit is done from the opposite side that **the** entrance is made. After the rope passes across the floor and proceeds to lift up into the arch the student leaps out with the flow of the rope and "exits" to the side.

1. *The twirlers swing the rope back and forth across the floor* without describing an arch and the jumper jumps over the rope each time that it passes under his feet.

2. Same as 1 except that after a couple of half swings the twirlers should send the rope into a complete circle and the jumper jumps it.

3. During 1 and 2 the jumper should face one of the twirlers but now he should face outward with his side to the twirlers and execute the jumps with the rope describing complete circles.

4. *One leg jump combinations.* The jumper may try jumping the rope by hopping on both feet, then one foot and then alternating from one foot to the other. The jumper may also try spreading his legs, and so on.

5. *Doubles jumping.* Two students jump the rope at the same time.

6. *Complicated maneuvers.* Many complicated maneuvers may be attempted such as having a doubles team enter and exit a turning rope, having a student simply run through the rope with a fast entrance and exit, do the same except with a jump or two prior to exiting. A doubles team can work in tandem fashion in that the first person enters the rope and executes a skip or two and then exits with the second person entering just as the first person exits. Two persons might try entering, jumping, and exiting at the same time.

7. *Skipping along with jumping.* The student may try to skip an individual rope while jumping in the larger jumping rope. All the variations suggested for both single skipping and long rope jump-ing may be tried together in this phase of the activity.

8. *Circling rope.* One person in the center swings the rope along the floor in a wide circle. Any number of persons standing within the range of this circling rope must jump over the rope as it approaches them.

Rope Climbing

The activity of rope climbing can be very interesting and challenging in a modern physical education program. It is basically the activity of climbing up and down a vertical rope suspended from a support overhead. The rope should be 3″ Manila; secure it safely from beams overhead and place a mat under it. Knot the rope at the bottom to prevent fraying.

Rope climbing

In climbing for the first few times it is suggested not to climb too high. Just a few feet at a time will accustom the climber to the rope and the techniques involved. Be sure to learn to climb downward as well as upward. Never slide down the rope as this will burn the hands and legs severely.

Because of the tiring effect of this activity, it is advisable to limit the amount of time devoted to it. When first introducing the activity to the students, a full period might be devoted to it for demonstration and presentation of safety hints. Thereafter it is best when undertaken at the end of the period. Rope climbing at this time can serve to bring the group together and to motivate them to an all-out effort. Contests of various sorts can also be planned which will keep interest and enjoyment high.

The following list represents a progressive order of learning the art of rope climbing, finishing with the intricate skill of climbing the rope with the hands alone for speed. This latter method is what is specified for official competition.

1. *The activity of chinning* with legs either vertical or horizontal to floor.

2. *Start from a standing position,* climb two pulls (strokes) upward and lower slowly to a standing position. Increase the number of strokes upward with each try.

3. *From standing position,* hold onto rope and lower down to the mat to a supine position.

4. *From supine position,* pull up to a standing position.

5. *From supine position,* grasp rope and do chin-ups by pulling with the arms.

6. *From standing position,* lower hand over hand to a sitting position, pull back up to a standing position (legs receive no support from floor although touching it).

7. *From standing position,* grasp rope, flex the arms, and raise legs to L position (parallel to floor) and hold for two or three seconds. Increase holding time with each try.

8. *From standing position,* grasp rope and raise legs to an inverted hang position then lower slowly to standing position.

9. *Grasp rope and climb upward three to four strokes* and raise body to an inverted hang position.

10. *Climb upward using the foot and leg lock method.* In this method the rope passes between the legs and around the back of the right leg and across the instep of the right foot. Step on the rope with the left foot. Pull with the arms and allow rope to slide through and then make fast with the foot. From this clamp or lock position straighten the legs and reach upward with the arms for new grip. Climb and descend with this lock.

11. *Climb upward using the stirrup method.* In this method allow the rope to pass along the side of the body down along the leg and under the near foot and over the other foot. Grasp rope and pull knees up with the rope passing through this position. Clamp the feet together, hold body in position, straighten the legs while the hands reach upward for new grip.

12. *Climb upward using the cross leg method.* In this method allow the rope to pass down between the legs, over the instep of one foot and against the back of the other foot, clamp the two feet together while reaching upward for new grip.

13. *Using feet and hands climb upward for speed* ten to twenty feet (start from a standing position).

14. *Using hands only climb upward*

for speed ten to twenty feet (start from a standing position).

15. *Using hands and feet climb upward from sitting position* ten to twenty feet.

16. *Using hands only climb upward from sitting position* ten to twenty feet.

At times it may be desirable to hold a position on the rope in order to rest a few moments. Three hold or rest positions will be described here.

1. *Foot and Leg Lock Rest Position.* Climb rope using foot and leg lock method—at rest position hold the foot and leg lock on rope and pass right arm in front of rope so rope is along side of right side of body and back of right armpit. Circle both arms in back of body and grasp wrists. This position is held by applying foot and leg lock and squeezing right arm against rope.

2. *Inverted Hang Rest Position.* Climb upward to the rest position spot and swing legs upward to an inverted hang position. Place one leg in front of rope and one in back. Reach behind head with right hand and grasp rope and pull it across the back and in front of chest passing under left armpit. Squeeze with legs and arms and the position is accomplished.

3. *Single or Double Leg Seat Position.* Climb upward a few feet and then stop and reach down with either hand and pull rope up to rope above. Grasp both ropes and hold Seat Rest Position. The rope may pass between legs to make a single leg seat or may pass under both legs and make a double leg seat.

Two ropes close to each other can also be used in the climbing program; see photograph.

Competitive Rope Climbing

Competitive rope climbing is truly an art and skill by itself. It does not involve

Inverted hang on two ropes

all the intricacies and maneuvers of apparatus work yet the art of climbing can be detailed and exacting in nature. A great deal of practice is involved to produce a champion rope climber. Since the record for climbing a rope 20 feet high with the hands alone is under 3 seconds it is easily understood why considerable practice is necessary for top performances. With all this in mind the following paragraphs explain in detail the techniques of climbing the rope for speed:

Start standing on the floor with the rope in front of the body about arms' length away. Grasp the rope with the arms straight out from the shoulders. The hands should grip the rope with the back of the hands facing the climber. Lower the body to a sitting position on the floor so just the back side of the thighs touch the floor. The rope should continue to be in a vertical position with the body leaning slightly backward with the elbows bent a little. The take-off is the most difficult part of the climb and with this in mind the two hand pull should be very forceful and strong. After this initial pull of both arms continue to lean back with your upper body and look up towards the tambourine during the climb. Pull one hand down on the rope and continue the pull until that hand is near the hips and at the same time reach straight up with the other hand for the next pull. Try to avoid sweeping across the chest to grasp the rope and always keep your palms away from your body. Avoid a straight L position of the body during the climb but instead strive for an open L or almost open horizontal position of the body.

The legs add power and speed by kicking down just before the pull with the hand. The leg action should not be wild or exaggerated but instead should be smooth and controlled.

The number of strokes taken by the best climbers for the 20 feet is usually seven or eight and the reach. The reach should be made with a straight up motion. When practicing, the reach should always be made with the same hand so strength and general timing is perfected to the finest detail. A good reach should be more than three feet and closer to four. Only the fingertips need to touch and to pull beyond that height will add to the climber's time.

The best exercise for rope climbers is climbing itself. Each time the climber works out he should be timed several times for speed.

Tug of War

Another rope activity which involves some of the same action as rope climbing is a tug of war. Such contests are usually greeted with enthusiasm and interest from both participants and spectators. Teams may be composed of almost any number of members, and each one gets an equal amount of exercise. The only equipment that is needed is a rope that is the size of a climbing rope or larger and some marks on the floor or ground past which the front man must be pulled for the victory. A little teamwork in pulling will make up for the lack of some strength.

CHAPTER 16

The Springboard

Trampoline

THE SPRINGBOARD TRAMPOLINE is a recently invented piece of gymnastic equipment that is meeting with unanimous approval throughout the country. Commercially manufactured under such names as "Trampolet," "Mini-Tramp," and "Aqua Tramp," its purpose is that of a springboard.

Mechanically speaking, it consists of a rigid steel tubular ring about 3' in diameter or a square frame about 3' wide supported by legs and cushioned with rubber traction shoes which will grip smooth gym floors. The legs are adjustable so that the angle of the woven web bed may be changed to suit the performer. The woven web bed is suspended by rubber cables or springs. This provides a maximum bounce for the performer.

VALUES

The specific values of working on the springboard trampoline are:

1. Supplements or assists instruction in such activities as tumbling, diving, trampolining, cheerleading, and vaulting.

2. Fulfills the natural desire to jump into the air and execute various other expressive movements.

3. Develops agility, coordination, and balance as the performer learns to maneuver his body while in the air.

4. Because of its compactness and easy maneuverability it is an excellent device to use in staging exhibitions.

ORGANIZATION

Before elaborating on the many stunts that can be done on the springboard "tramp," a few basic safety hints should be mentioned.

1. Progress slowly in learning the use of the apparatus. The first few attempts should merely consist of bouncing off to the feet. Practice the art of leaning forward or backward, depending on the stunt in mind.

2. The springboard tramp may be padded with mats for safety. This is especially effective when first trying

stunts with it. As skill is developed the mats may be eliminated.

3. Use the safety belt in attempting somersaults for the first time.

4. Be sure the mechanical phases of the device are always in readiness: all shock cords securely fastened, rubber pads on the legs secure, adjusting screws tightened, and so on.

5. In spotting the activity have two spotters standing one on each side of the tramp to assist the performer through the first few attempts at the particular stunt.

6. When used to assist in tumbling or as an activity by itself, the springboard tramp might be placed on mats so that the landings can be on mats.

PROGRAM OF INSTRUCTION

The springboard trampoline may be employed in many ways: for tumbling, diving, cheerleading, vaulting, and so on. Before elaborating on these, a detailed program of instruction will be presented for activity with the device alone.

The art of simple bouncing off the springboard tramp is learned in much the same way as the approach and take-off on a diving board. The performer merely trots toward the apparatus and just prior to reaching it, lifts one leg up followed immediately with the other and leaps onto the bed of the tramp. This acts as the hurdle. Upon landing on the bed the performer sinks downward, and the recoil of the rubber cords sends him into the air for the execution of the stunt.

At the time of the bounce the arms are lifted into the air and the head and chest are raised also. Diligent practice is needed to master the basic technique of bouncing off the springboard tramp for only then can the many fine and enjoyable stunts be performed.

1. *Ball-Up.* This stunt is a slight variation of simply bouncing forward off the tramp. Upon taking off bring the knees up to the chest and momentarily grasp the shins; this ball-up or tuck position is assumed for a split second then released and the legs extended downward in preparation for the landing on the mat.

Ball-up

2. *Straddle Touch.* The performer upon leaving the tramp leaps into the air and extends the legs forward and to the sides in a straddle position. The toes are touched lightly with the hands and then the legs are snapped downward to the mat. This takes practice though, so it is suggested that the performer try touching the knees first, then the shins, and finally the ankles or toes.

3. *Half Twist.* Take off from the tramp in a forward bounce. While taking off, start a half-turn to the right by pulling the right shoulder back. Look in the

Straddle touch

direction of the turn and execute the half twist. Land on the feet facing the tramp.

4. *Full Twist.* This is similar to the half twisting jump except that a complete full turn is executed before landing on the mat. Be sure to keep the body straight while twisting. Also don't twist too hard off the tramp as this will cause the body to tilt and an improper landing will result.

5. *Half Turn on Tramp.* This stunt consists of bouncing straight up off the tramp and executing a quick half twist landing back on the bed and then bouncing off to the feet in the direction of the original run.

6. *Backward Bounce Stunts.* For the most part the stunts listed above such as straight forward leap, tuck bounce, straddle touch, half twist, clap hands, and so on, may also be tried going backward from the tramp. Be sure to get the

proper lean backwards so that the feet clear the frame upon landing.

7. *Leap to Feet into Forward Roll.* Leap forward from the tramp and land on the feet and then go into a neat forward roll. Be sure to emphasize to the students that they must land squarely on the mat with their feet before starting the forward roll.

8. *Leap Backward to Feet into Backward Roll.* Bounce backward from the tramp and land on the feet and then go into a quick backward roll.

9. *Bounce Twice on Tramp into a Backward Leap.* Bounce straight up on the first rebound and then hit the bed again with the feet and lean back slightly to a backward bounce to the feet. Try this stunt first from an extremely low bounce. On second bounce be sure to anticipate the backward leap so that the feet will clear the frame upon landing on the mat.

After the fundamentals of bouncing have been taught and the performer feels at home on the springboard tramp, it may be used effectively to assist in instruction in other areas or to use as a performance in itself. Some of these areas are as follows:

Tumbling

It is a fine device with which to assist the tumbler in executing his somersaults, twisters, and so on. Some suggested stunts are:

Over the low or back end:

1. Back somersault—tuck, pike, or layout position.
2. Hand balance on high end, kick-down, back somersault.
3. Back somersault with half twist.
4. Back somersault with full twist.

Back somersault (tuck)

Back somersault with half twist

Back somersault (layout)

Back somersault with full twist

Over the high or front end:

1. Front somersault—tuck, pike, and layout.
2. Barani.
3. Gainer.
4. Front somersault with full twist.
5. Front somersault with one and a half twist.

Front somersault (tuck)

Though these tumbling stunts are generally executed in a gym onto mats, they're also great fun on a sandy beach. This type of apparatus has been used a great deal at famous Santa Monica Beach in California.

Cheerleading

The apparatus is extremely valuable to a tumbling cheerleading squad. It aids tremendously in executing tumbling stunts in cheerleading routines. Because of its compactness, the springboard trampoline can be transported quite easily from game to game.

Diving

The device can be used quite effectively for diving practice. By using the overhead safety belt, many "dry-land" dives can be tried with comparative ease. It can also be used as a substitute for a diving board alongside a swimming pool or on a pier.

Trampoline Mounting

Trampoline performers can use the device as a means of mounting onto the trampoline. In exhibition, this method of mounting is particularly effective. Some of these mounts are:

1. Swan dive to a front drop.
2. Swan dive over to a back drop.
3. High bounce to a feet bouncing position—with half, full twist.
4. High bounce to a seat drop.
5. High bounce with a half twist to a back drop.
6. Back pullover out of stunt 5.
7. Front somersault.
8. Barani.
9. Front one and a quarter somersault to a front drop.
10. Front one and a quarter somersault with a half twist to back drop into back pullover.
11. Front one and three quarters somersault to a back drop.

Stunts for Two Performers

Two people can use the apparatus very effectively in staging exhibitions of tumbling and balancing skills. Some of these stunts are:

1. Bounce to a swan dive to a catch.
2. Bounce to shoulder mounts.
3. Bounce to high arm to arm balance.
4. Bounce to hand-to-hand balances.

Vaulting

The device can be used for vaults over such apparatus as long horse, buck, side horse, and parallel bars (covered with mats). A few of the vaults that can be done are flank vaults, front vault, rear vault, squat vault, straddle vault, headspring and handspring.

Mounting to the shoulders

CHAPTER 17

Gymnastic Exhibitions

A GYMNASTIC EXHIBITION is a display of the imagination and productivity of the students and teachers, limited somewhat though it may be by what is available at the particular school in terms of equipment, talent, space, time, and various other determining factors. Some schools with unlimited facilities can stage large productions while others with limited facilities will have to be content with smaller productions calling for greater ingenuity. It is the plan of this chapter to present some general ideas which might be helpful in planning any exhibition.

VALUES

Some of the values of gymnastic exhibitions are:

1. Offers the opportunity to demonstrate to the community some of the activities that are included within the physical education program.

2. Provides recognition for the boys and girls who are not participating in varsity sports.

3. Provides a school project in which many students are involved. This may bring greater unity to the school in that several departments and teachers of the school might cooperate in the staging of the entire production.

4. Provides a fine means of gaining some money for worthwhile school projects.

5. Provides an entertaining show for the community to witness.

Gymnastic exhibition in progress

ORGANIZATION

Gymnastic exhibitions can be of several types, depending upon their purposes. They may be simply to provide a short period of entertainment for the half-time at a basketball game. Occasionally entertainment is requested for a social engagement, and this, too, will be a limited performance of gymnastics skills. Often gymnastics performances will occupy a large portion of physical education demonstrations or community recreation programs. In many cases gymnastics will provide the entire program of entertainment in itself. Following are some suggestions for preparing a full length show.

Outside show for the community

Planning

Planning is definitely the key word to a successful gymnastic exhibition.

Extensive planning must be done early and involves considerable thought and direction by the teacher-director and his or her committee.

Committee Assignments

The initial work on any production is to divide your staff, class leaders, and students into various committees. People placed on these committees should be those who have indicated a keen interest in the show and are willing to work diligently on it. The director should appoint an assistant as this will save him the burdensome task of making all the decisions. To avoid further confusion it is suggested that each committee chairman be given a copy of the tentative program with a detailed list of instructions to be followed. The successful show depends upon each committee's fulfilling its obligations on time. A series of time deadlines for each committee should be worked out in order to keep things moving at a regulated pace.

Theme

One of the first items upon which to decide is the theme. Pick out a particular theme for each show and build the entire production around it. Some themes that have been used successfully by schools include: Physical Panorama; Sight Seeing Tour to Foreign Lands; Daze in Tulip Land; Fantasy Land; Toyland Capers; Playland, USA; and Out of This World.

Length of Show

The duration of your show should be approximately one and a half hours; it should not exceed two hours. It might be wise for the production committee to consider including a 15 minute intermission to break up the program.

Publicity

With the publicity committee rests the major responsibility of stimulating interest in attending the big show. Some means of creating this interest and enthusiasm are as follows:

1. Mimeographed flyers may be made and distributed to all the students and to members of the community.

2. Posters advertising the show may be made and placed in convenient or strategic places.

3. News articles covering all the details of the show along with photographs of some of the acts might be distributed to the local newspapers.

4. Spot announcements on radio and television might be possible in some areas.

Tickets

The ticket committee has a very important position in the production of the show. Through consultation with the director this committee proceeds to set the price of the tickets and arranges for the printing and distribution of them at the various purchasing sites. This should all be done two or three weeks prior to the show.

Costumes

The costume committee has a very difficult task to perform in that each costume should be attractive and in theme and yet kept to a minimum of expense. Whenever regular physical education activities are demonstrated, it is suggested that the regular gym outfit be used. The specialty numbers generally call for a different outfit. These might be made by the student involved, his or her mother, or perhaps by the home economics department of the school. All costumes should be approved by the committee chairman and the director of the show. None should be designed or cut so as to receive criticism from the parents or patrons.

Decorations

Decorations create the atmosphere for any type of performance and are an essential factor in a successful production. Gymnasia are rather difficult to decorate, but any change of scenery will be an added attraction for the audience.

The stage is set

Property

Since numerous pieces of equipment and props must be moved about throughout the show it is imperative that a good property manager and crew be obtained. Many times this committee can make or break a show.

Concessions

Another source of revenue in addition to tickets is the concession stand. Items such as popcorn, candy, soft drinks, and so on can be sold by the refreshment committee. Small extra revenue might also be obtained by posting a clown or two in the lobby of the building to sell canes, flags, pennants, or other souvenirs. It is suggested that balloons or other noise making items not be sold.

Printed Program

When the schedule of acts has been decided upon, a committee should begin working on a well designed printed program. This program may or may not carry advertisements, depending upon the policies of the school. The program should list the entire agenda along with the names of the participants and committee members. For public relations purposes, some of the administrative staff of the school and outstanding townspeople might be given special invitations and then listed as honored guests.

Program Schedule

Although the program is quite variable and flexible, some principles to follow in planning and arranging your acts are presented here:

1. A parade which should include all participants is nice to use as the opening event.

2. Use the smaller children early in the program.

3. Acts involving beginners should be at the early part of the program so that a climax of advanced skills may be reached at the end of the show.

4. For variety, acts involving groups of performers should be mixed in with acts involving individuals or small groups of two or three.

5. For variety, mix up the types of numbers. For example, a fast, snappy mass tumbling act would be good following a slow, precise doubles balancing routine. Also, if the program includes more than gymnastic acts, these differ-

ent activities should be intertwined with each other.

6. Interspersed throughout the program short comedy skits might be included. These might be simple clown acts or comedy gymnastic routines.

7. Any lengthy delay between acts should be avoided. If a delay is necessary for reasons such as moving equipment, comedy skits could be used to fill in the time.

8. An intermission of about fifteen minutes is advisable if the program is of considerable length. This allows for the moving of heavy equipment and props as well as concession stand sales.

9. An act including the entire cast should be used as the finale.

PROGRAM OF INSTRUCTION

Most of the gymnastic acts will involve stunts learned as part of the regular classroom instruction, just as described in the other chapters of the book. Since it is important that comedy be included in some of the gymnastic acts, the following routines and stunts are suggested for the various pieces of apparatus. They represent those that have been either used or seen by the authors. Perhaps they will stimulate ideas in the development of more of this type of stunt.

Not everyone is suited to be a comedian so be careful in casting these roles. Although it is essential that the clown wear a uniform that is different and funny, he must also have a personality that is suited for clowning. The comedian should also be a good performer since many of the funny stunts require special skill.

Tiger Leaping

This involves long horse vaulting with

Doubles balancing act

the use of a springboard. The group should be comprised of six to ten vaulters including the comedian. The general pattern is for the vaulters to follow one another in close order, with the comedian bringing up the rear. The vaulters should start with the easier stunts such as straddle vaults or squat vaults and gradually work up to the more difficult vaults such as cartwheels, headsprings and handsprings. The comedian's routines may be as follows, keeping in mind that he is last in each series of vaults:

1. Hesitate as if bewildered and afraid to do the stunt but finally be persuaded to start the run. Immediately prior to reaching the springboard, veer off to one side and run past the equipment and circle back to the starting position.

2. Run toward the springboard, take a high hurdle but miss the end of the board and land between the board and the horse with the end of the horse touching the abdomen.

3. Run up the springboard onto the horse and off the front end.

4. Follow the last two vaulters, attempting to imitate their headspring off the neck. Instead do a forward roll into a lying position on the neck with the

arms and legs circling the horse. As soon as this position is reached, the other vaulters should straddle vault over the clown. When the last vaulter has completed his vault, slide off the horse and run back to the starting place.

5. A proficient tumbler may do a complete front somersault over the long horse. Emphasize poor form and clutch hat to head while sailing through the air.

6. Finish the tiger leaping act by stacking several men on the neck of the horse. Build this up gradually, one man at a time and when four or five or more men are piled up, do a straddle vault over all of them.

Tumbling and Balancing Stunts

This group could comprise six to ten tumblers including the comedian. The general pattern of action on the tumbling mats is for the tumblers to follow one another down the mat. They should start with the easier stunts such as forward rolls and cartwheels and gradually work up to the more difficult stunts such as flip-flaps, somersaults, and twisters.

1. *Routine.* In this, as in tiger leaping, the comedian should be the last one for

each trip down the mat. The routines for the comedian might be as follows:

a. Follow the last tumbler by simply running straight down the mat as if a difficult stunt is to be done but never do it.

b. Do a series of cartwheels and tinsicas and then walk off the mat as if extremely dizzy.

c. After all the tumblers have executed successful dives and rolls over each other in a kneeling position, prepare to dive over the entire group. Audience participation may be obtained by asking for volunteers to kneel in between the tumblers. This is especially successful if children are in the crowd. After much preparation run up to first man but instead of diving over, run across the buttocks of all the kneeling persons.

d. Follow a tumbler who does a forward roll into a somersault or some such forward stunt and do a similar routine, but instead of completing the somersault out of the forward roll go only three-fourths of the way and land squarely on the buttocks with the legs extended straight ahead. Jump up and run off holding the "injured" portion.

e. Have two tumblers and comedian straddle-jump over and forward roll under each other. Comedian jumps higher and faster than the other two.

f. If comedian is a proficient tumbler finish your performance with a good "straight" series of flip-flaps, somersaults, twisters, and so on.

2. *Newspaper Dive and Roll.* A person is sitting on a low stool reading a magazine. Another person does a high dive over the first person, grabbing the magazine as he goes over and then executes a roll with the paper in his hands. He may either end up sitting on the mat or continue rolling to a standing po-sition. In either case he ends up reading the magazine nonchalantly.

3. *Broom Swing Flip.* During an argument between two people, the one person swings a broom at the other one. The broom should be swung low at the legs. As the broom approaches the legs, the non-swinger does a back flip thus allowing the broom to pass under him without touching him.

4. *Wobbly Low Hand to Hand.* Comedy can be worked into a doubles hand balancing stunt quite nicely such as a low hand to hand. It involves the bottom man presenting a shaky support as the top man attempts to kick up into a balance position. The bottom man should be very relaxed and loose when the top man attempts to get into position. After some maneuvering to get the bottom man's arms solid, perform the stunt in the regular manner.

Horizontal Bar Stunts

Not many stunts of the comedy nature can be done on the horizontal bar. A couple of them will be described here. In addition to these, synchronized work done in opposite directions by two performers may be quite entertaining. Simple routines not involving stunts causing the performer to move along the bar will be suitable. Such a routine might be: back uprise, back hip circle, underbar swing, single knee swing up, single knee circle backward, kip, underbar swing, hock swing dismount.

1. *Barber Pole.* Jump up and grasp one of the vertical standards with one hand. The jump should be with a slight forward motion so that the performer will rotate around the bar in a circular direction. By slowly releasing the grip, the performer will gradually descend

as he rotates. One or two complete revolutions is usually sufficient to produce laughs.

2. *Double Hip Circles.* This stunt requires two performers. The first man does a belly grind mount. The second man grasps the bar inside of his partner's hands and pulls his legs up as if doing the same stunt. However, he spreads his legs and hooks them behind his partner's back. The second man is now upside down. After a little rocking motion, they start into a backward hip circle. Halfway through the hip circle, the second man is upright and on top while the first man is underneath and upside down. The performers may pause here and then continue the action for a few more circles or do several circles in rapid succession.

3. *Straddle Stoop Gag.* While one man swings on the high bar another man walks beneath the bar and stoops as if picking up a piece of chalk or some such object. Timing should be such that the man stoops as the high bar performer swings through straddling his legs to avoid hitting him. This provides for a quick and exciting comedy gag.

Parallel Bar Stunts

Many comedy stunts are possible on the parallel bars. Several of them involve falling which requires careful attention and much practice to avoid injuries.

1. *Scratching Leg.* When holding a hand balance (or shoulder balance) casually scratch the calf of one leg with the toes of the other. It is best to scratch with the leg nearest the audience.

2. *Lazy Man's Kip.* This stunt is described in the parallel bar chapter as a leadup stunt to the ordinary kip on the end of the bars. However, it can be used as a comedy stunt if the clown does it immediately following a performance of an ordinary kip by a fellow gymnast.

3. *Walking into the Bars.* This stunt may be used by the clown in pretending that he doesn't see the bars while walking along. Just before he supposedly hits his chin or head on the bar, he kicks one foot up in front of him, and places his hands by the buttocks to brace himself when he falls on his back beneath the bars. Sound effects would be effective if carefully timed.

4. *Hock Swing Fall.* A hock swing dismount may be done from the parallel bars by lifting the legs between the bars and hooking them over one bar. From this position, perform the stunt as on the horizontal bar. The comedy part comes in releasing the legs too soon and landing on the stomach between the bars. Of course, most of the weight of the body is absorbed by the hands and arms as they hit the mats first. This may be more effective if preceded by a straight performer actually completing the stunt.

5. *Collapse.* From a straddle seat position relax completely and fall backward, releasing the grasp as you fall. The legs remain hooked over the bars as long as possible in order to lessen the force of the fall. If the body is kept straight, it will swing as in the hock swing dismount, and the ending can be a fall on the chest.

6. *Stoop-Kick.* This stunt involves two performers. One has just finished a stunt at the end of the bars and is slow leaving, because he stoops to pick up an object or to look at the mat closely. The second performer may either jump to an upper arm support or do a backward giant roll. With proper spacing and timing, the second performer's feet swing

forward and kick the buttocks of the stooping first performer thus causing him to lunge forward and fall.

7. *Arm Slide.* This is done by a performer wearing a long-sleeved shirt. The performer either takes a running jump to an upper arm support or does a fast backward giant roll. In either case he releases his grasp and allows the momentum to slide him on his arms along the bars. The slide may even continue to the end and off from the bars where the performer could land on his buttocks on the mats.

8. *Tickle Gag.* A gymnast maneuvers himself into a bird's nest position below the bars, holding on to the rails with his feet and hands. Maintaining that he is stuck, he calls for help from his fellow gymnasts. One or two proceed to push, pull, and shove him off the bars. Nothing seems to work, though, until one person holds up his hand as if to say "Ah, I've got the solution." Then he moves in close to the gymnast and "tickles" his stomach with his fingers, which causes him to drop to a prone position on the mats below.

Trampoline Stunts

The trampoline is very much suited to comedy stunts. A little imagination can produce many funny routines because of the various ways a person may fall and bounce without getting injured. No attempt will be made to present all of the known comedy stunts. Instead a few will be described as representative of the various types possible.

1. *Step Through Springs.* When attempting to mount the trampoline, the performer steps through the springs. This is best done by running towards one corner where the most clear area for stepping is available. A good gag to accompany this is to pretend to mash the face against the tramp bed after stepping through. By carrying a few beans in your mouth, one can spit them out as if they were teeth that had been knocked out.

2. *Rope Pull from End.* From a position of sitting on the end frame bar with the legs braced under the springs and tramp bed, comedian falls backwards so that his body is parallel to the tramp bed. He pretends that someone from the other end has thrown him a rope and is pulling him up. He raises his body slowly by applying pressure on the tramp bed with the feet and occasionally slips back before coming to an upright position and mounting the trampoline.

3. *Suicide Dive.* From a high bounce, straighten the body and dive head first for the bed. Of course, duck your head before landing and land on your shoulders and back. A screaming noise might add to the excitement of this stunt.

4. *One Leg Dive.* At the top of the bounce, the performer bends over and grabs one leg, allowing the other leg to swing backward parallel to tramp bed. As he nears the bed, he releases his grasp and straightens out his body, landing in a front drop.

5. *Waving Turntables.* While doing a series of turntables, look and wave at the audience each time around.

6. *Low Back Drops.* Do a series of back drops and get lower on each one. Then you can pretend you are pulling on a rope and gradually raise the height of each back drop until you end in a standing position.

7. *Back Walk Over.* Do a backward three quarters somersault to a front drop. As you are doing the flip, move your feet as though walking.

8. *Highest Back Flip.* Start bouncing and work up to as high a bounce as you

can. Then kill the bounce and immediately do a very low back flip. Prepare for this stunt by announcing that you are going to do the highest back flip in the world. While bouncing, encourage the audience to shout "Higher!" with each bounce. Then the very low flip comes as a complete surprise.

9. *Basketball Bounce.* This stunt is done by two performers. The first performer does a back drop in a tuck position and remains in that position after the bounce. The second performer pushes the first performer into another back drop as though bouncing a basketball. Repeat the stunt several times.

10. *Straddle Over.* This stunt is done by two performers. The first performer bounces high with his legs in a straddle position. The second performer walks underneath while the first performer bounces. When walking underneath he looks at the audience and waves at someone. Repeat this sequence a second time. On the third time, the man walking underneath only walks through halfway, pretending to be interested in something in the audience. Suddenly he looks up and sees his partner coming down on top of him. He lets out a shriek and does a back drop while the bouncer straddles him. The audience thinks the bouncer has landed on him.

Selected List of Reference Materials and Visual Aids

BOOKS

Burns, Ted, and Tyler Micoleau, *Tumbling Techniques Illustrated.* New York: Ronald Press, 1957.

Cotteral, Bonnie, and Donnie Cotteral, *The Teaching of Stunts and Tumbling.* New York: Ronald Press, 1936.

Davidge, Bernice, and William J. Quinn, *Elementary Tumbling and Stunts.* Langstaff, Ontario: David G. Smith, 1957.

Field, David A., *A Manual of Selected Exhibitional Gymnastic Activities.* College Park, Maryland: University of Maryland, 1951.

Fischer, Hugo, Dean R. Shawbold, and Paul R. Wohlford, *Individual and Dual Stunts.* Minneapolis: Burgess Publishing Co., 1950.

Griswold, Larry, *Trampoline Tumbling.* St. Louis: Fred Medart Manufacturing Co., 1948.

Horne, Virginia Lee, *Stunts and Tumbling for Girls.* New York: Ronald Press, 1943.

Kunzle, G. C., and B. W. Thomas, *Olympia Gymnastic Series* (seven books). London: James Barrie Books Ltd., 1957.

LaDue, Frank, and Jim Norman, *This is Trampolining.* Cedar Rapids, Iowa: Nissen Trampoline Company, 1954.

LaPorte, William Ralph, and Al G. Renner, *The Tumbler's Manual*. Englewood Cliffs, New Jersey: Prentice-Hall, Inc., 1944.

Lienert, Walter J., *The Uneven Parallel Bars*. 233 N. Parkview Ave., Indianapolis, Indiana, 1957.

Loken, Newt, *Beginning Tumbling and Balancing* (1951), *Advanced Tumbling and Balancing* (1958), *Trampolining* (1958), *Gymnastics for Girls and Women* (1958), *Apparatus Activities for Boys and Men* (1958). "How to Improve" series, numbers 1-5, respectively. Chicago: The Athletic Institute.

———, *Trampolining* (revised). Ann Arbor: University of Michigan, 1958.

Loken & Gagnier, Ed., *Sequence Gymnastics*, University of Michigan, 1959

Miller, Charles E., *Physical Training—Practical Suggestions for the Instructor*. St. Louis: Fred Medart Products, Inc., 1949.

Price, Hartley D., Joseph M. Hewlett, and Newt Loken, *Gymnastics and Tumbling* (revised). New York: Ronald Press, 1950.

Ryser, Otto, *Teacher's Manual for Tumbling and Apparatus Stunts* (Second Revised Edition). Dubuque, Iowa: Wm. C. Brown Co., 1951.

Scannell, John, *A Manual of Heavy Apparatus and Tumbling Stunts*. Minneapolis: Burgess Publishing Co., 1956.

Szypula, George, *Tumbling and Balancing for All*. Dubuque, Iowa: Wm. C. Brown Co., 1957.

West, Wilbur D., *The Gymnast's Manual*. Englewood Cliffs, New Jersey: Prentice-Hall, Inc., 1942.

PERIODICALS

The following periodicals contain articles and information regarding gymnastics:

Amateur Athletic Union Gymnastics Yearbook
233 Broadway, New York 7, New York

Athletic Journal
1719 Howard Street, Evanston, Illinois

Journal of Health—Physical Education—Recreation
1201 16th St., N.W., Washington 6, D.C.

The Mentor
P.O. Box 425, Arlington, Texas

The Modern Gymnast
P.O. Box 611, Santa Monica, Calif.

Newsletter of the National Association of Gymnastics Coaches
c/o Newt Loken, University of Michigan, Ann Arbor, Michigan

Physical Educator
3747 N. Linwood Ave., Indianapolis, Ind.

Scholastic Coach
33 West 42 St., New York 36, N. Y.

VISUAL AIDS

Film Strips. The following 35 mm. film strips, similar in content to the Loken "How to Improve" series of books cited above, are available from the Athletic Institute, 209 South State Street, Chicago 4, Illinois: 1. Beginning Tumbling and Balancing; 2. Advanced Tumbling and Balancing; 3. Apparatus Activities for Boys and Men; 4. Trampolining; 5. Gymnastics for Girls and Women.

Loop Films. The following series of loop films are available:

Champions on Film
303 S. Main,   1. *Trampolining*
Ann Arbor, Michigan·   2. *Tumbling*

16mm. Motion Pictures. The following is a list of motion pictures available, classified according to source of supply:

AAU Motion Picture Library
223 Broadway   *The Official AAU Gymnastic Championship Meets*
New York, New York

Audio-Visual Aids Center
University of Michigan   *Handstand to High Bar*
Ann Arbor, Michigan

Castle Films Division
1445 Park Avenue   *Tumbling for Physical Fitness*
New York, New York

Coronet Instructional Films
Coronet Building,   1. *Beginning Tumbling*   3. *Advanced Tumbling*
Chicago, Illinois   2. *Intermediate Tumbling* 4. *Simple Stunts*

Encyclopedia Brittanica
1150 Wilmette Avenue   *Headsprings in the Gym*
Wilmette, Illinois

Film Exchange Committee
Milton Berkowitz, Chairman   *Olympic, World Championship, and*
47 Boyd Avenue   *Sarasota Clinic Films*
Jersey City, New Jersey

NCAA Office
209 Fairfax Building   *NCAA Gymnastic Meet Films*
Kansas City 5, Missouri

Nissen Trampoline Co.
200 A Avenue N.W.
Cedar Rapids, Iowa

1. *Up in the Air*
2. *Whatever Goes Up*

Paul Hoefler Productions
612½ South Ridgely Drive
Los Angeles 36, California

1. *Gymnastics—Fundamentals and Techniques*
2. *Gymnastics—Fundamentals and Techniques*

Photographs. A set of photos for the horizontal bar, parallel bars, long horse, and tumbling-calisthenics is available from: Frank Endo
12200 S. Berendo
Los Angeles 44, California

Index

A

B

C

C